Creating
Visual Studio LightSwitch Custom Controls
(Beginner to Intermediate)

Published By

The LightSwitch Help Website

http://LightSwitchHelpWebsite.com

Copyright

Table of Contents

Dedication

As always, for Valerie and Zachary

Preface

Requirements

You must have Visual Studio Professional 2010 (or higher) to create Silverlight Custom Controls using the methods described in this book.

To complete the examples in chapters 3 and 4, you will need to install the **Silverlight Toolkit** available at: http://silverlight.codeplex.com.

To complete the examples in chapter 5, you will need **Microsoft Expression Blend 4** (or higher) see: http://www.microsoft.com/expression/products/blend_overview.aspx. If you do not have Expression Blend, you can download the completed code from http://LightSwitchHelpWebsite.com.

Intended Audience

You are familiar with, and you are creating applications using **Visual Studio LightSwitch** (http://www.microsoft.com/visualstudio/en-us/lightswitch).

If you are new to using LightSwitch, it is suggested that you start with this tutorial: http://lightswitchhelpwebsite.com/Blog/tabid/61/EntryId/12/Online-Ordering-System-An-End-To-End-LightSwitch-Example.aspx

You do not need to have prior experience or knowledge of Silverlight, or Silverlight Custom Controls.

Thank You

I apologize if I forget anyone, but I would like to thank the following people:

Karol Zadora-Przylecki
Steve Hoag
Sheel Shah
Joe Binder
Beth Massi
Michael Eng
Robert Green
John Rivard
Steve Anonsen
John Stallo
Jay Schmelzer
Alessandro Del Sole

Open Light Group (http://OpenLightGroup.org):

Ian Lackey
Richard Waddell
Haruhiro Isowa
Alan Beasley

Chapter 1: Enhancing LightSwitch "Why Do I Want To Make A LightSwitch Silverlight Custom Control?"

You have decided to make LightSwitch Silverlight Custom Controls for your LightSwitch application. The first question to answer is, why? Perhaps for the following reasons:

- You want to display data to your users in a visually captivating way, such as with the use of charts and graphs.
- You want to use non-standard user controls to allow for the easier input of data, such as the use of sliders.
- You require your users to perform a multiple-step process, and you want the screen to change based on the current step.

The difference between a Silverlight Custom Control and a LightSwitch Control Extension

It is important to note the difference between a Silverlight Custom Control, and a LightSwitch Control Extension.

Karol Zadora-Przylecki covers the difference in the article "Using Custom Controls to Enhance Your LightSwitch Application UI" (http://blogs.msdn.com/b/lightswitch/archive/2011/01/13/using-custom-controls-to-enhance-lightswitch-application-ui-part-1.aspx). Essentially the difference is that a LightSwitch Control Extension is installed into LightSwitch, and meant to be re-used in multiple LightSwitch applications, like a normal internal LightSwitch control. The downside is, that creating a LightSwitch Control Extension, is significantly more difficult and time-consuming to create.

Silverlight Custom Controls are controls created specifically for the LightSwitch application they will be implemented in. They are significantly easier to create. Silverlight Custom Controls will be covered in this book.

When You Need A Silverlight Custom Control

When we look at the **Online Ordering System** sample from **LightSwitchHelpWebsite.com** (http://lightswitchhelpwebsite.com/Blog/tabid/61/EntryId/12/Online-Ordering-System-An-End-

To-End-LightSwitch-Example.aspx), we see an application that allows us to associate orders and order details.

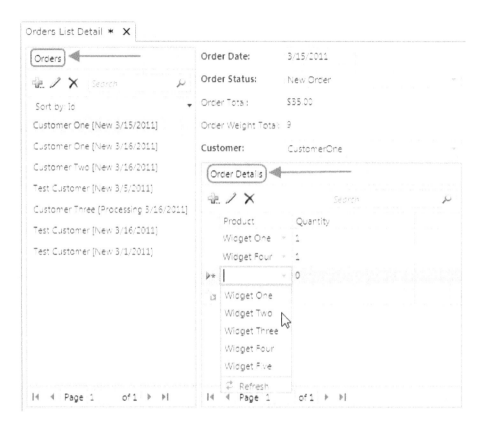

LightSwitch is very useful, and easy to use, when displaying data in related tables.

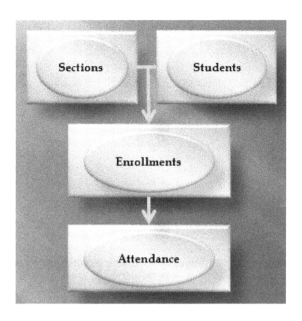

However, when faced with a business use case such as the one illustrated above, where you need to relate multiple Entities (tables) to allow the user to record Attendance, while LightSwitch will allow you to perform the functionality, it may not present an optimal solution.

The picture above shows the screen that LightSwitch will allow you to create to enter Attendance data. While this will achieve the objective, it is less than desirable because:

- You must enter the Attendance Code, Date, and Enrollment each time
- It is not easy to see the Attendance already entered

In "the real world", a Teacher is usually sitting in front of a class (a Section) and is looking at the Students. In this situation, the Teacher knows what Section it is, and what day it is.

To be most effective, the Teacher wants to see a list of all the Students who are Enrolled in the class on that day (they do not want to see any Students who have dropped the class), and they want to quickly mark the Attendance for the Students.

The image above demonstrates how a Silverlight Custom Control can be used to achieve the objective in an intuitive way.

The Silverlight Custom Control is able to display the Student, The Enrollment, and the Attendance for the day, at one time. In addition, the user is able to change the Attendance by a single click on a radio button. LightSwitch does not contain a control that will naturally do this.

Chapter 2: Get the Data
"How LightSwitch Implements MVVM"

First let us discuss, what is MVVM?

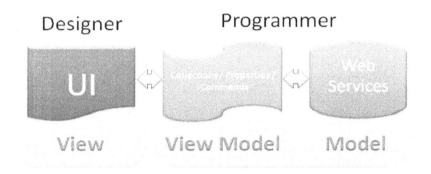

This article, **Silverlight View Model Style: An (Overly) Simplified Explanation**
(http://openlightgroup.net/Blog/tabid/58/EntryId/89/Silverlight-View-Model-Style-An-Overly-Simplified-Explanation.aspx), explains what MVVM is. Basically:

- **Model** – The Data
- **View Model** – Collections, Properties, and Commands
- **View** – The UI (User Interface)

The Model

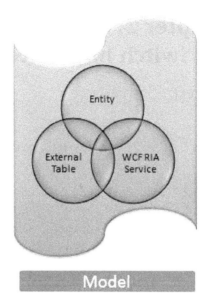

The Model is where the data for the application goes. The Model is composed of:

- Entity – An internal LightSwitch table. These are called Entities because they can contain fields or properties that are calculated, and may not actually be part of the underlying SQL Server table.
- External Table – Data sources you create in LightSwitch by connecting to an external table.
- WCF RIA Service – Any data source that consists of a WCF RIA Service.

The View Model

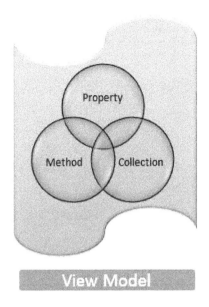

View Model

The View Model consists of:

- Properties – One of something. This could be a String or an Object. Implements INotifyPropertyChanged, so that any element bound to it, is automatically notified whenever it changes.
- Collections – A collection of something. This is of type ObservableCollection, so that any element bound to it, is automatically notified whenever it changes.
- Methods – Code that is called by an event.

The View

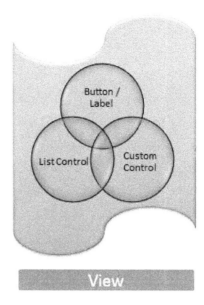

The View consists of any User Interface element. In LightSwitch, the View also includes any Silverlight Custom Control.

The reason we want to cover MVVM, is that when implementing any Silverlight Custom Controls in LightSwitch, we must first understand how LightSwitch binds Silverlight Custom Controls to data in our LightSwitch application.

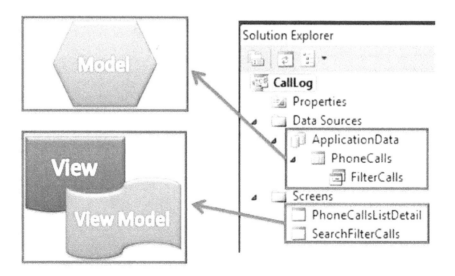

The Model, the data, is considered to be any data source in a LightSwitch application. If you have created a table in LightSwitch, you have created a Model.

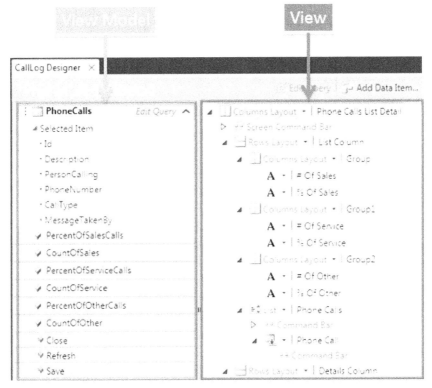

With LightSwitch, you create the View Model, by placing Properties, Collections, and Methods (normally Methods are called Commands. As far as the "MVVM pattern" is concerned, they are the same thing because they serve the same purpose), on the *left-hand* side of the screen designer.

On the *right-hand* side of the screen, you bind UI elements, (either the build-in LightSwitch controls, control extensions, or Silverlight Custom Controls), to those Properties, Collections, and Methods.

LightSwitch binds Silverlight Custom Controls to the View Model just as it would any other LightSwitch control.

Chapter 3: Chart Viewer
"Binding Silverlight Custom Controls"

There are various ways to bind a Silverlight Custom Control to Properties, Collections, and Methods in a LightSwitch View Model. In this chapter, we will explore all of them with the "Chart Viewer" sample application.

Note: We will demonstrate how a Silverlight Custom Control can call a method in a LightSwitch View Model in Chapter 5 of this book.

*Note: To complete the examples in this chapter, you will need to install the **Silverlight Toolkit** available at: http://silverlight.codeplex.com.*

You can download all the code referred to in this book, from the "Downloads" page on http://LightSwitchHelpWebsite.com.

Create The Sample Project

Create a new LightSwitch project.

Make a **Sale** table, with the schema according to the image above.

Create a **SalesPerson** table with the schema according to the image above.

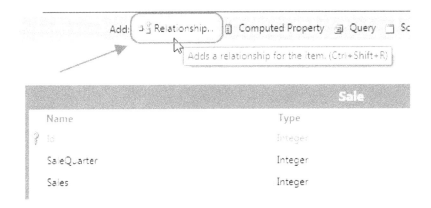

Open the **Sale** table, and click the **Relationship** button.

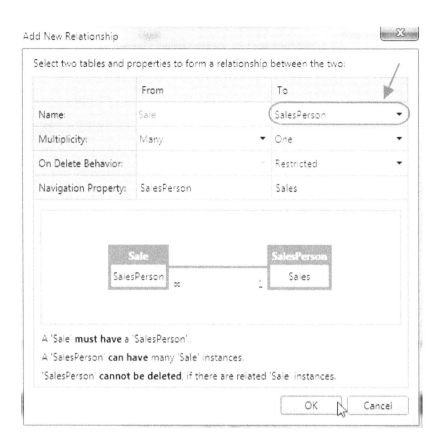

Create a relationship to the **SalesPerson** table and click **OK**.

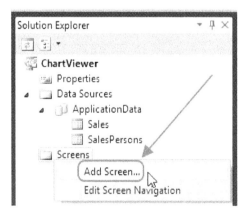

Right-click on the **Screens** node in the **Solution Explorer**, and select **Add Screen…**

Create a **List and Details Screen** using the settings in the image above.

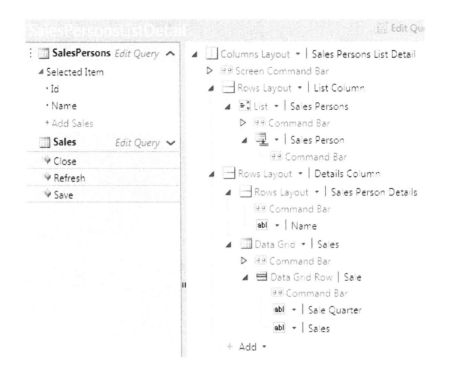

The screen will display in the designer.

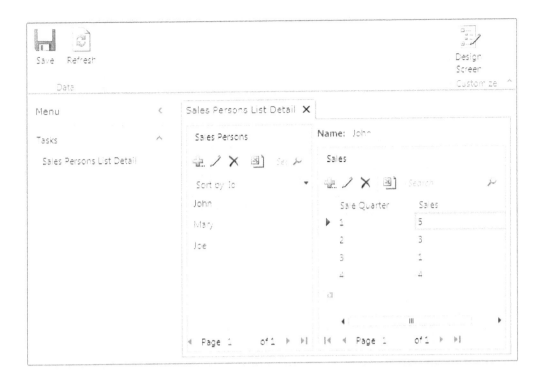

Press the **F5** button to run the application, and enter sample data (enter sales data for 4 quarters for each sales person).

After entering data, close the window to stop the application.

Create The Silverlight Project

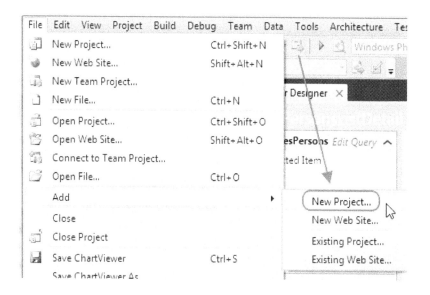

Add a **New Project** to the solution.

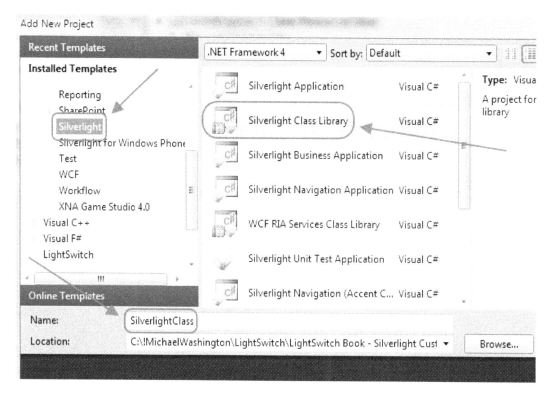

Create a new Silverlight project, and call it **SilverlightClass**.

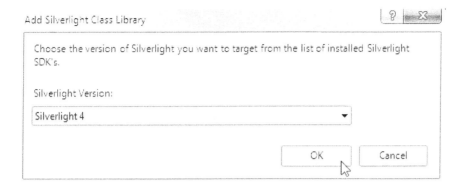

Make it a **Silverlight 4** project.

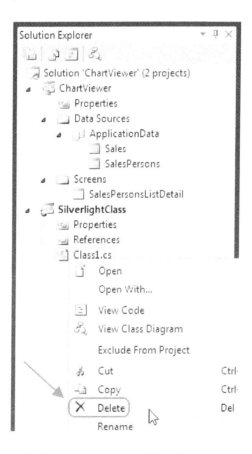

Right-click on the **Class1.cs** file that is created, and delete it.

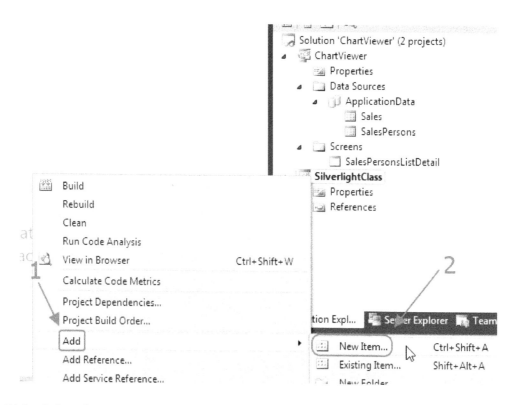

Right-click on the **SilverlightClass** project, and select **Add** then **New Item…**

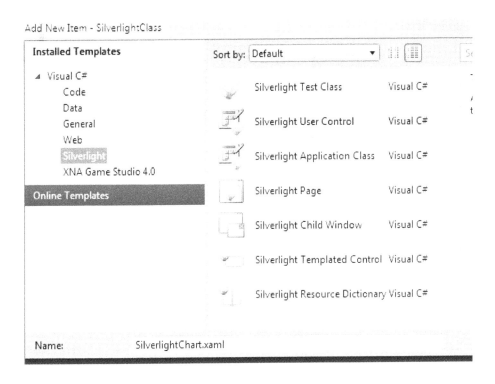

Create a **Silverlight User Control**, and name it **SilverlightChart.xaml**.

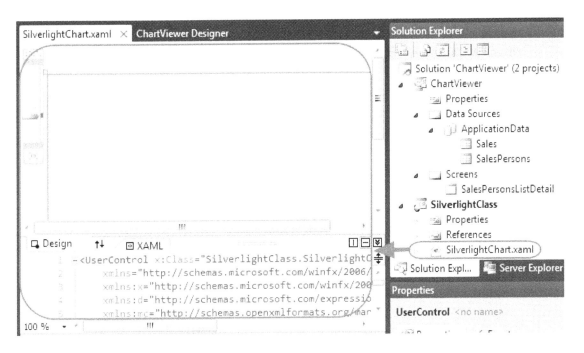

The control will show up in the project, and the code will open in the design window.

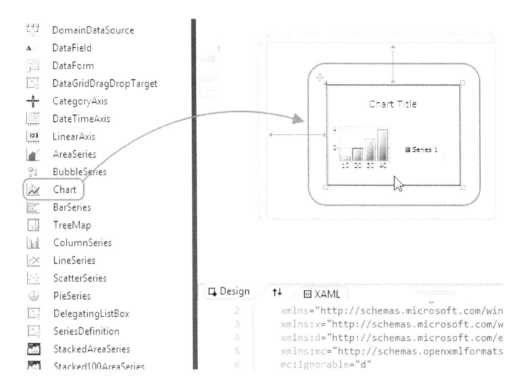

Drag the **Chart** control from the **Visual Studio Toolbox**, to the design surface of the **SilverlightChart.xaml** page.

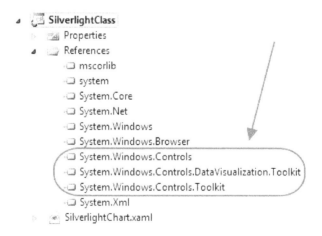

This will automatically add the required assemblies to the project.

```
1   <UserControl x:Class="SilverlightClass.SilverlightChart"
2       xmlns="http://schemas.microsoft.com/winfx/2006/xaml/presentation"
3       xmlns:x="http://schemas.microsoft.com/winfx/2006/xaml"
4       xmlns:d="http://schemas.microsoft.com/expression/blend/2008"
5       xmlns:mc="http://schemas.openxmlformats.org/markup-compatibility/2006"
6       mc:Ignorable="d"
7       d:DesignHeight="300" d:DesignWidth="400"
8               xmlns:toolkit="http://schemas.microsoft.com/winfx/2006/xaml/presentation/toolkit">
9
10      <Grid x:Name="LayoutRoot" Background="White">
11
12          <toolkit:Chart Name="SalesChart">
13              <toolkit:Chart.Series>
14                  <toolkit:BarSeries Title="Sales" ItemsSource="{Binding Screen.Sales}"
15                                     IndependentValueBinding="{Binding SaleQuarter}"
16                                     DependentValueBinding="{Binding Sales}"/>
17              </toolkit:Chart.Series>
18              <toolkit:Chart.Axes>
19                  <toolkit:CategoryAxis Title="Sales Quarter" Orientation="Y" FontStyle="Italic"/>
20              </toolkit:Chart.Axes>
21          </toolkit:Chart>
22      </Grid>
23
24  </UserControl>
```

Change the code, to the code above.

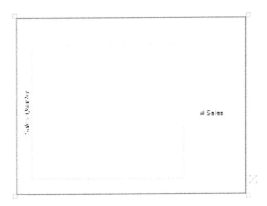

The control will resemble the image above.

Note: If you see XAML display errors in the Visual Studio page designer, closing and re-opening the .xaml page will clear them up. If you continue to receive errors, download the completed project from http://LightSwitchHelpWebsite.com and compare it to your own code.

```
="SalesChart">
  Series>
  rSeries Title="Sales" ItemsSource="{Binding Screen.Sales}"
              IndependentValueBinding="{Binding SaleQuarter}"
              DependentValueBinding="{Binding Sales}"/>
  :.Series>
  Axes>
  itegoryAxis Title="Sales Quarter"
                Orientation="Y" FontStyle="Italic"/>
  :.Axes>
```

The Silverlight custom control markup contains binding directives. Note that bindings can be one of three types:

- **One Way** - LightSwitch can change the underlying value, but the Silverlight Custom Control cannot change the value in LightSwitch.
- **Two Way** - LightSwitch can change the underlying value, and the Silverlight Custom Control can change the value in LightSwitch.
- **One Time** – LightSwitch can set the underlying value one time.

If the binding type is not specified (in our example it is not), the binding will be **One Way**.

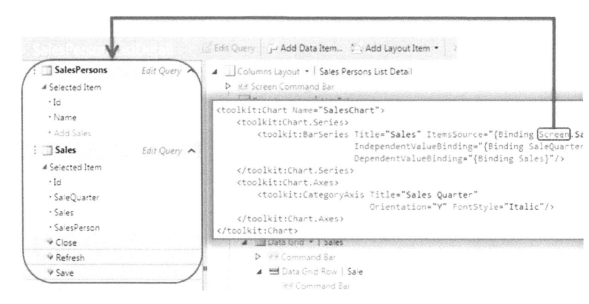

The main binding is to the LightSwitch screen. The **View Model** is on the *left hand* side of the LightSwitch screen designer. In binding with Silverlight Custom Controls, it is referred to as "**Screen**".

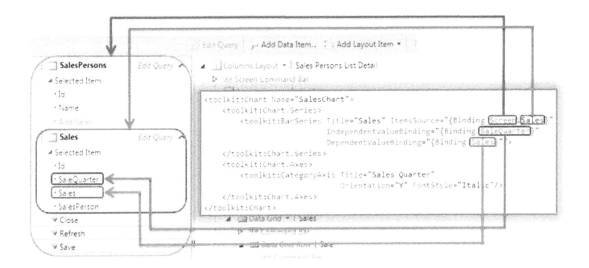

The complete binding is illustrated above.

Insert The Custom Control Into LightSwitch

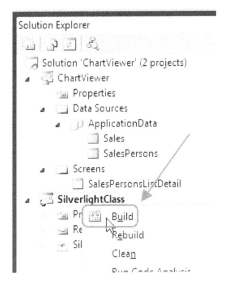

Build the project.

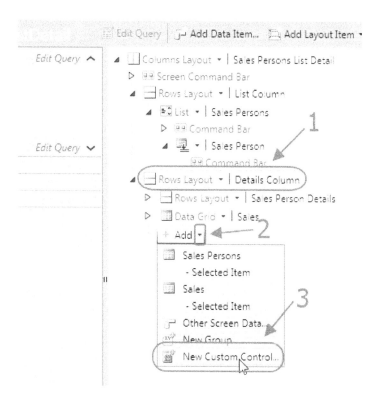

In the LightSwitch screen designer, select the **Details Column** and add a **New Custom Control**.

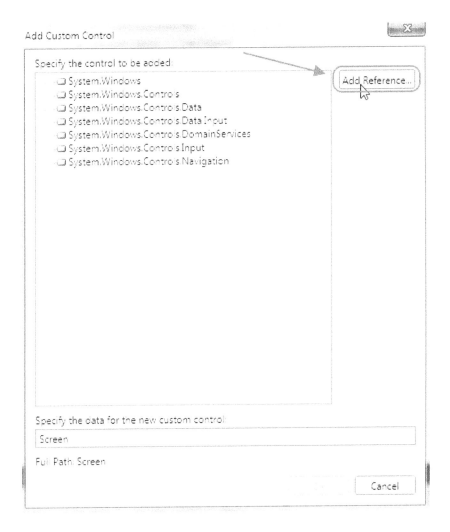

Add a **Reference**.

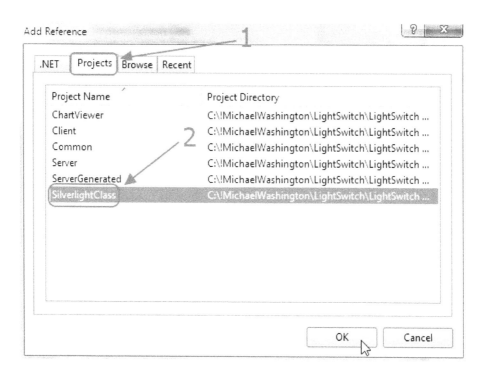

Select the **SilverlightClass** project.

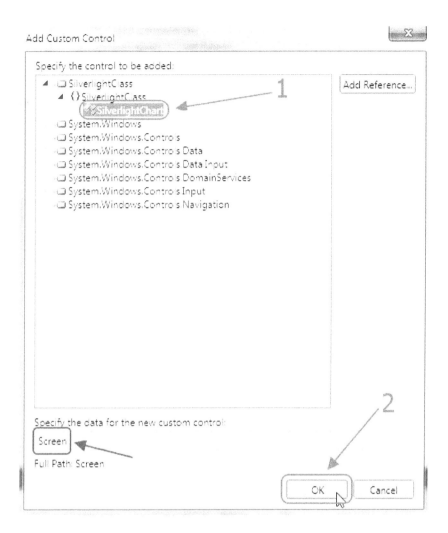

Select the **SilverlightChart** control.

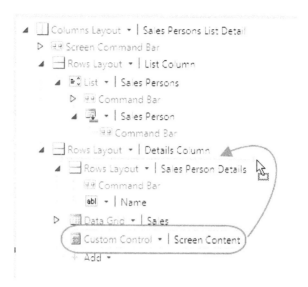

Drag the control, to move it to the top of the **Details Column**.

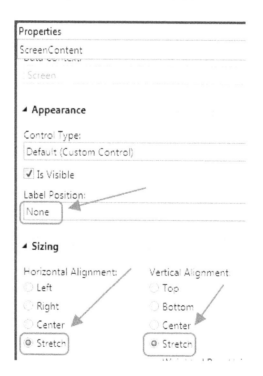

In the Properties for the Custom Control, set the **Label Position** to **None** (so it won't show), and set the alignment to **Stretch**.

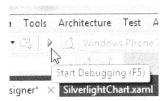

Run the project.

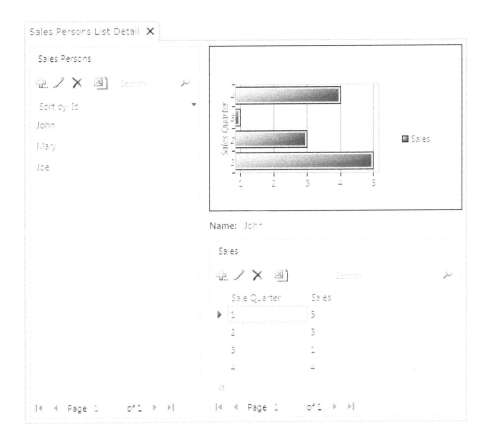

The chart will display.

Two Way Binding

In the next example, we will demonstrate **Two Way** binding using sliders. We will also explore three methods to bind Silverlight Custom Controls in LightSwitch.

In this example, we will use slider controls to change the sales quarter being displayed. To do this, we will need a query that accepts a parameter to set the sales quarter.

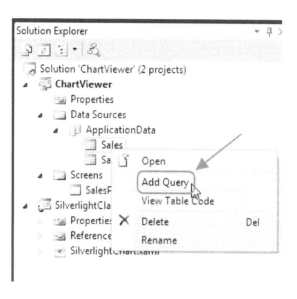

Right-click on the **Sales** entity in the **Solution Explorer**, and select **Add Query**.

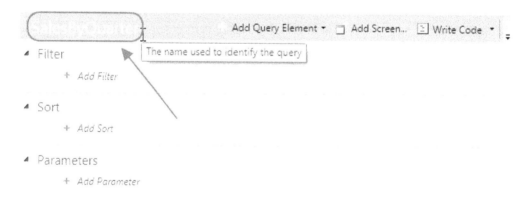

In the query designer, click on the name, to change the name of the query to **SalesByQuarter**.

Add a **Where** clause, and select **SaleQuarter** as the field to query.

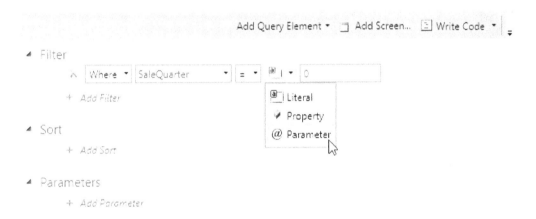

Specify a **Parameter**.

Add a new **Parameter**.

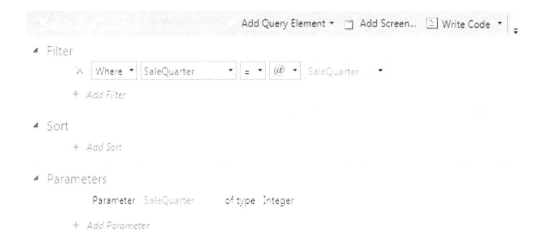

Name the **Parameter SaleQuarter**.

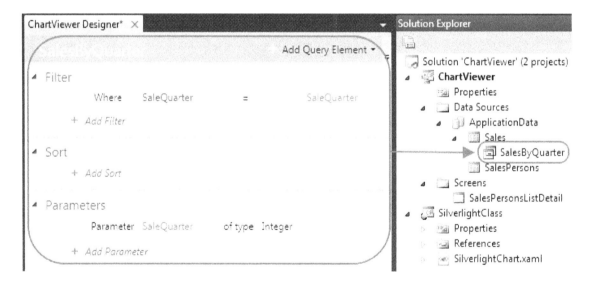

Click the **Save** button.

The **SalesByQuarter** query will show in the **Solution Explorer**.

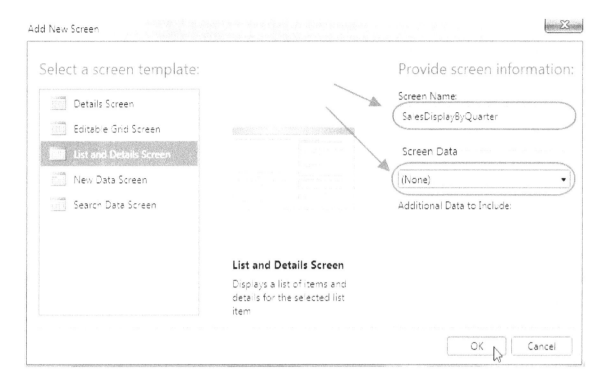

Select a screen template:

- Details Screen
- Editable Grid Screen
- **List and Details Screen**
- New Data Screen
- Search Data Screen

List and Details Screen

Displays a list of items and details for the selected list item

Provide screen information:

Screen Name:

Sa esDisplayByQuarter

Screen Data

(None)

Additional Data to Include:

OK   Cancel

Create a new screen using the **List and Details Screen** template, with **(None)** selected for **Screen Data**.

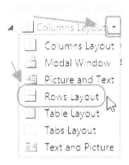

- Columns Layout
- Columns Layout
- Modal Window
- Picture and Text
- Rows Layout
- Table Layout
- Tabs Layout
- Text and Picture

Change the layout to **Rows Layout**.

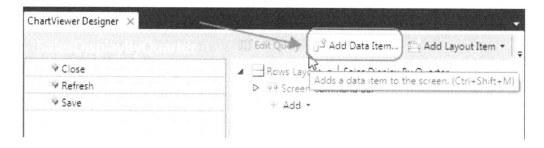

Add a **Data Item** to the screen.

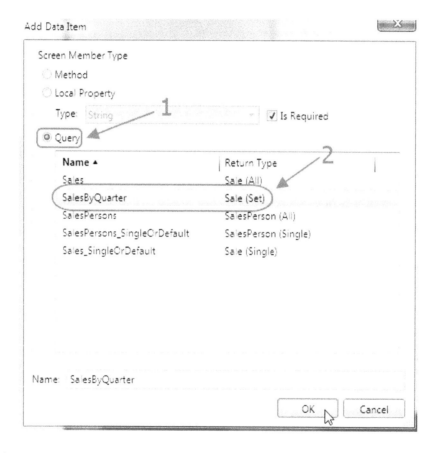

Select the **SalesByQuarter** query created earlier.

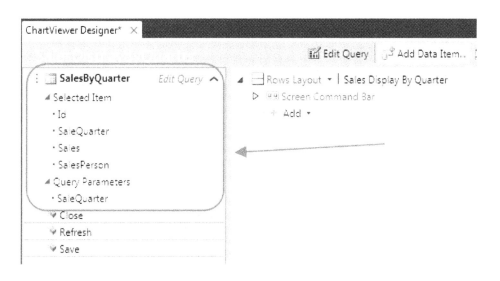

The collection will show in the **View Model** for the screen.

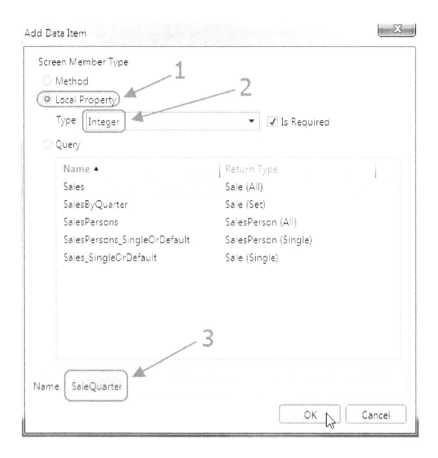

We now need to create a parameter to pass to the query. Add an **Integer** property to the screen, and call it **SaleQuarter**.

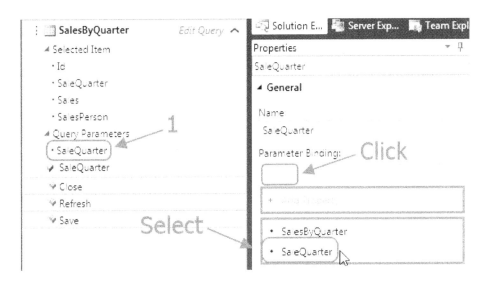

Bind the **SaleQuarter** property to the parameter in the **SalesByQuarter** collection, by clicking on the **SaleQuarter** parameter, and clicking in the **Parameter Binding** box, in the properties for the parameter. Then select **SaleQuarter**.

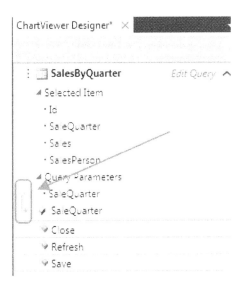

You will know that you have bound the parameter correctly, when you see an arrow connecting the parameter to the property, when you click on the property.

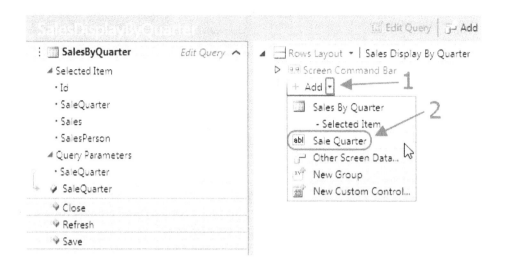

We want to display the parameter on the screen (it will be set by sliders created in later steps).

Add the **Sale Quarter** parameter to the screen. Note, when we bound the parameter in the previous step, the 'display name' was set as 'Sale Quarter' (with a space).

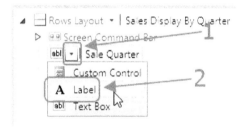

Initially it will be a **Text Box**, change it to a **Label**.

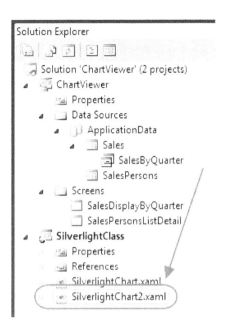

Add a new Silverlight Control called **SilverlightChart2.xaml**.

```xml
<UserControl xmlns:sdk="http://schemas.microsoft.com/winfx/2006/xaml/presentation/sdk"
             x:Class="SilverlightClass.SilverlightChart2"
             xmlns="http://schemas.microsoft.com/winfx/2006/xaml/presentation"
             xmlns:x="http://schemas.microsoft.com/winfx/2006/xaml"
             xmlns:d="http://schemas.microsoft.com/expression/blend/2008"
             xmlns:mc="http://schemas.openxmlformats.org/markup-compatibility/2006"
             mc:Ignorable="d"
             d:DesignHeight="300" d:DesignWidth="400"
             xmlns:toolkit="http://schemas.microsoft.com/winfx/2006/xaml/presentation/toolkit">

  <Grid x:Name="LayoutRoot" Background="White">

    <toolkit:Chart Name="SalesChart">
        <toolkit:Chart.Series>
            <toolkit:BarSeries Title="Sales" ItemsSource="{Binding Screen.SalesByQuarter}"
                              IndependentValueBinding="{Binding SalesPerson}"
                              DependentValueBinding="{Binding Sales}"/>
        </toolkit:Chart.Series>
    </toolkit:Chart>

  </Grid>
</UserControl>
```

Use the code above.

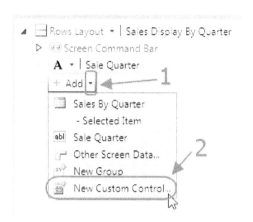

Build the project. Add a **New Custom Control** to the screen.

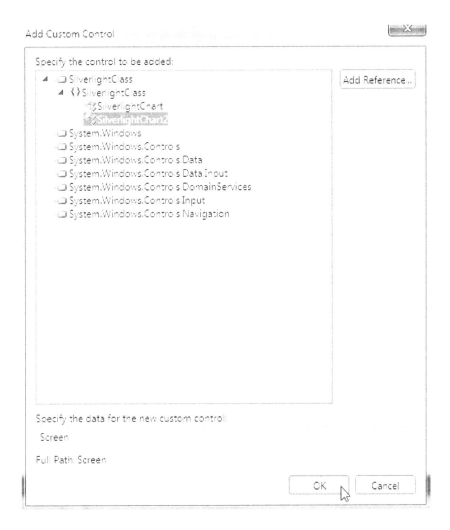

Select **SilverlightChart2**.

In the properties for the chart, set the **Alignment** to **Stretch**.

Method One: Directly Binding A Silverlight Control

The first method we will explore, is binding a Silverlight Control assembly (a .dll) programmatically.

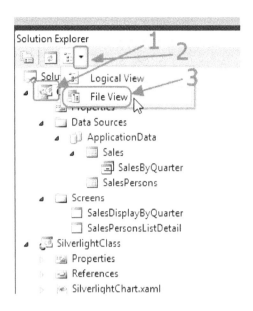

First, click on the LightSwitch project in the **Solution Explorer**, and select **File View**.

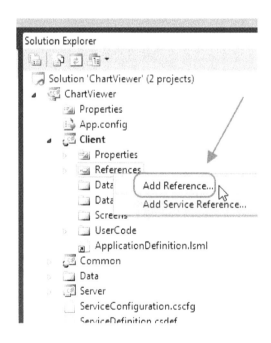

Select **Add Reference**…

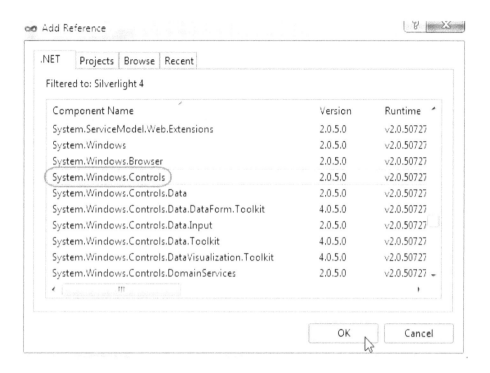

… to **System.Windows.Controls**. We do this because we will make a direct reference to the **Slider** control that is contained in that assembly.

In the screen designer, add a new **Custom Control**.

Select the **Slider** control under **System.Windows**, then **System.Windows.Controls** (do not go to *System.Windows.Controls* first, because it will not be under that tree node).

Enter **SaleQuarter** as the data to bind to.

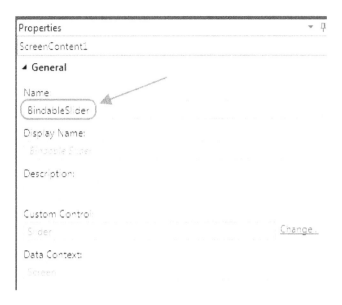

In the properties for the control, set the name to **BindableSlider**.

Set the **Horizontal Alignment** to Stretch.

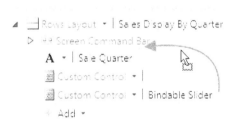

Drag the control to the top of the screen.

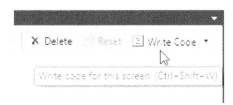

Select **Write Code**.

```
using System;
using System.Linq;
using System.IO;
using System.IO.IsolatedStorage;
using System.Collections.Generic;
using Microsoft.LightSwitch;
using Microsoft.LightSwitch.Framework.Client;
using Microsoft.LightSwitch.Presentation;
using Microsoft.LightSwitch.Presentation.Extensions;
using System.Windows.Controls;
using System.Windows.Data;

namespace LightSwitchApplication
{
    public partial class SalesDisplayByQuarter
    {
        partial void SalesDisplayByQuarter_Created()
        {
            // Write your code here.
            this.SaleQuarter = 1;

            var ctrlProxy = this.FindControl("BindableSlider");
            ctrlProxy.SetBinding(Slider.ValueProperty, "Value", BindingMode.TwoWay);
            ctrlProxy.ControlAvailable +=
                new EventHandler<ControlAvailableEventArgs>(ctrlProxy_ControlAvailable);
        }

        void ctrlProxy_ControlAvailable(object sender, ControlAvailableEventArgs e)
        {
            // Remove Control Handler
            this.FindControl("BindableSlider").
                ControlAvailable -= ctrlProxy_ControlAvailable;

            // Set defaults for Slider
            Slider SliderControl = e.Control as Slider;
            SliderControl.Maximum = 4;
            SliderControl.Minimum = 1;
        }
    }
}
```

Change the code to the code above.

This code uses **SetBinding** to bind the control to "Value". "Value" is **SaleQuarter** that we set when we added the Custom Control in the **Add Custom Control** dialog.

This code also creates a handler that will fire when the control is ready. Because Silverlight does not create a control until it is needed on the screen (for example the user may need to scroll down to see the control), we cannot assume the control is immediately available. When the control is "available" we set additional parameters on the control.

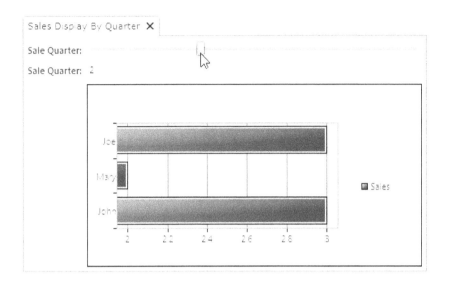

When you run the application, you will be able to move the Slider and change the **Sales Quarter** that is displayed.

Method Two: Using Value Binding For A Silverlight Control

In this example, we will bind a Slider using a .xaml Silverlight Custom Control. However, we will code the binding in LightSwitch rather than in the XAML code.

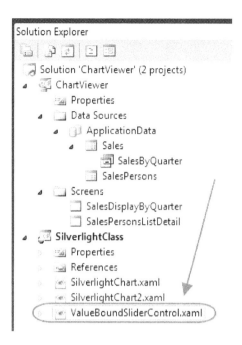

In the **SilverlightClass** project, create a new Silverlight Custom Control called **ValueBoundSliderControl.xaml**.

```xaml
<UserControl x:Class="SilverlightClass.ValueBoundSliderControl"
    xmlns="http://schemas.microsoft.com/winfx/2006/xaml/presentation"
    xmlns:x="http://schemas.microsoft.com/winfx/2006/xaml"
    xmlns:d="http://schemas.microsoft.com/expression/blend/2008"
    xmlns:mc="http://schemas.openxmlformats.org/markup-compatibility/2006"
    mc:Ignorable="d"
    d:DesignHeight="300" d:DesignWidth="400">

    <Grid x:Name="LayoutRoot" Background="White">

            <Slider Value="{Binding Path=Value, Mode=TwoWay}"
                    Maximum="4"
                    Minimum="1"
                    SmallChange="1" />

    </Grid>
</UserControl>
```

Use the code above.

```
e="{Binding Path Value, Mode=TwoWay}"
num="4"
```

Notice that the binding path is just "Value". Also, notice the **Mode** is set to **TwoWay**.

Build the project.

Add a new Custom Control to the **SalesDisplayByQuarter** screen. When you add it, as with the previous Slider, set the binding path to **SaleQuarter**.

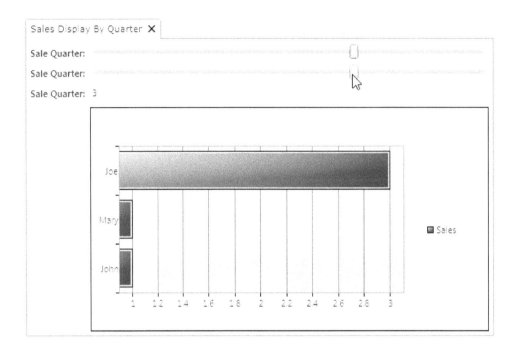

When you run the project, the Slider will work.

Method Three: Explicit Binding Of A Silverlight Control

The last method is just like the method used for the Silverlight Chart controls. The only difference is that it uses **Two Way** binding.

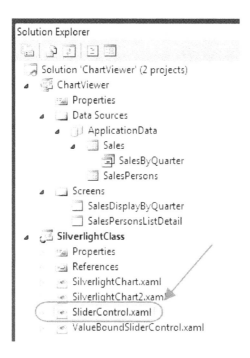

Create a new Silverlight Custom Control called **SliderControl.xaml**.

```xml
<UserControl x:Class="SilverlightClass.SliderControl"
    xmlns="http://schemas.microsoft.com/winfx/2006/xaml/presentation"
    xmlns:x="http://schemas.microsoft.com/winfx/2006/xaml"
    xmlns:d="http://schemas.microsoft.com/expression/blend/2008"
    xmlns:mc="http://schemas.openxmlformats.org/markup-compatibility/2006"
    mc:Ignorable="d"
    d:DesignHeight="300" d:DesignWidth="400">

    <Grid x:Name="LayoutRoot" Background="White">

        <Slider Value="{Binding Path=Screen.SaleQuarter, Mode=TwoWay}"
                Maximum="4"
                Minimum="1"
                SmallChange="1" />
    </Grid>
</UserControl>
```

Use the code above. Notice it uses the full binding, including specifying "**Screen.**".

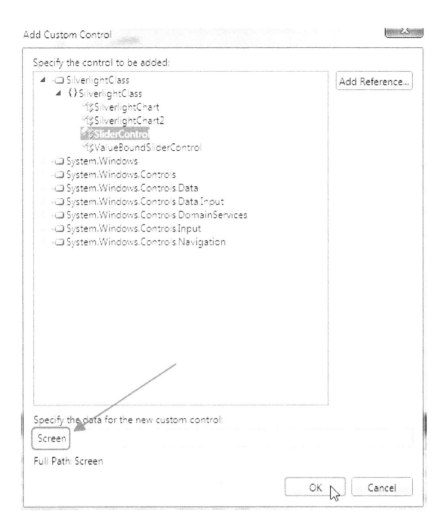

When you add the Custom Control to the Screen, leave the default "**Screen**" as the binding.

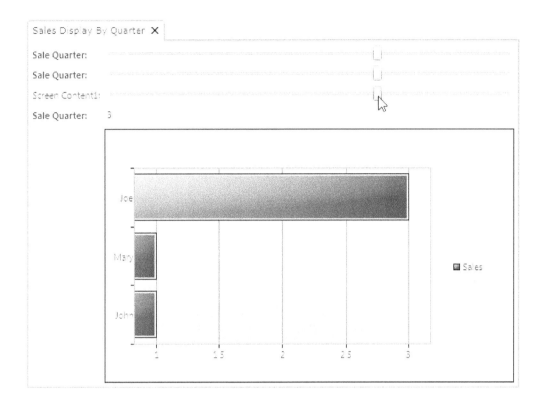

The final project will have 3 sliders with slightly different bindings that perform the exact same function.

Chapter 4: Chart Viewer
"Creating In-Memory Records"

You will find a slight problem with the chart in the preceding chapter. If a sales person does not have any sales for a quarter, they will not appear on the chart at all.

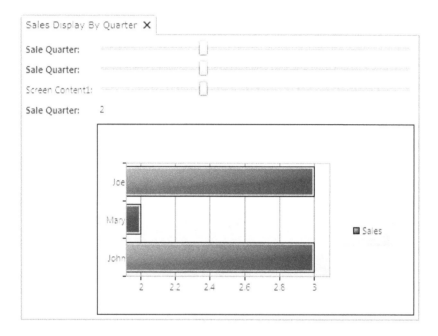

In Sales Quarter 2, all three sales people have sales, therefore each sales person appears on the chart.

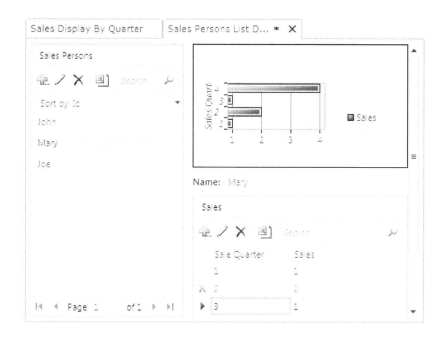

However, delete the 2nd quarter sales for Mary (remember to click save).

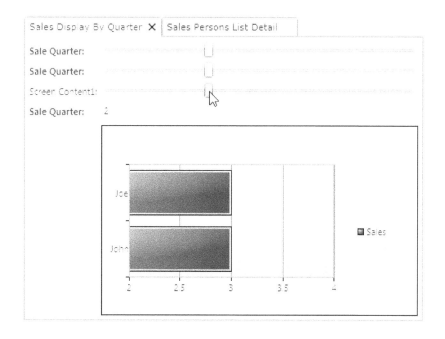

When we return to the **Sales By Quarter** page (and click **Refresh** to update the data with the latest changes), we see that Mary is entirely absent from the chart for that sales quarter.

LightSwitch is designed to require you to create each new record you want, as a new record. Only then can you represent the data on the screen. We have a screen that shows the sales data for the second quarter. Mary has no sales, so Mary does not show.

What we sometimes desire, is for LightSwitch to create "blank spots". We would like to see Mary on the chart (but with sales of 0).

While this scenario is not exclusive to Silverlight Custom Controls, it will most likely come up, because, when you are creating Silverlight Custom Controls, you want the screen to appear exactly how you desire.

First, Get All the Data You Need On The Screen

This first step is not obvious. You will need to place all the collections you will need on the screen, even if you do not plan to show all the collections on the screen.

However, remember that by default all collections are set to only contain 45 records at a time. You will want to turn paging off, in the Properties for the collection, if you need to access all records in a collection programmatically.

To resolve our particular challenge, we need to determine what sales people do not have sales data for the selected quarter. This requires us to query the **SalesPerson** entity, and the sales of each person to see if they have sales for the selected quarter.

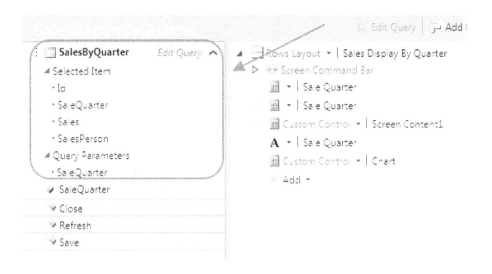

Currently we have the **SalesByQuarter** query on the screen. The problem with just using this query, is that it has already filtered the sales people, to only those sales people that have sales for the quarter.

We need a collection that provides access to all the sales people.

Add the **SalesPerson (All)** collection to the screen.

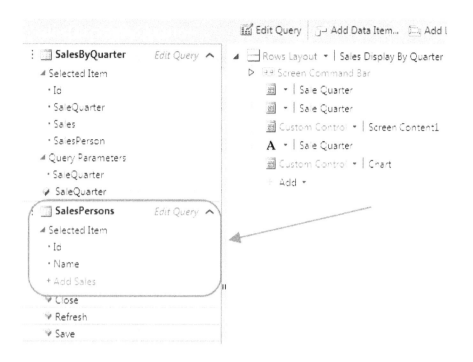

We now have programmatic access to the collection.

Again, remember that by default this collection will only contain 45 records. You will want to turn off paging, in the Properties for the collection, to have programmatic access to all the records.

Create In-Memory Records

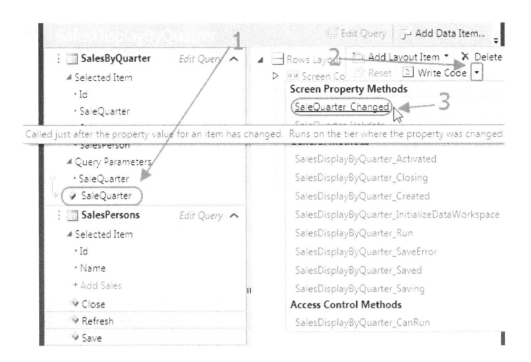

The next step is to wire-up a method to fire whenever the **SaleQuarter** parameter is changed. Click on the **SaleQuarter** parameter in the View Model for the screen, and then select **SaleQuarter** changed to create the method.

```
int intLastSalesQuarter = -1;
partial void SaleQuarter_Changed()
{
    // Check to see if the Quarter actually changed to prevent looping
    if (intLastSalesQuarter != this.SaleQuarter)
    {
        intLastSalesQuarter = this.SaleQuarter;

        // Remove any unsaved Sales
        foreach (Sale sale in this.DataWorkspace.ApplicationData.Details.GetChanges()
            .AddedEntities.OfType<Sale>())
        {
            sale.Details.DiscardChanges();
        }

        // Get all SalesPersons who do not have Sales for the Quarter
        int[] intSalesPersonsWithoutSales = (from objSalesPersons in SalesPersons
                                        where objSalesPersons.Sales.
                                        FirstOrDefault(x => x.SaleQuarter
                                            == SaleQuarter) == null
                                        select objSalesPersons.Id).ToArray();

        int intTempID = -1;
        // Loop through the SalePersons
        foreach (int item in intSalesPersonsWithoutSales)
        {
            // Get the SalesPerson record
            SalesPerson objSalesPerson =
                DataWorkspace.ApplicationData.SalesPersons_Single(item);

            // Create a Sale for the SalesPerson
            Sale objSale = objSalesPerson.Sales.AddNew();

            objSale.Sales = 0;
            objSale.SaleQuarter = SaleQuarter;
            objSale.SalesPerson = objSalesPerson;
            // we need to give each record a unique ID
            // So we insert negative numbers and count backwards
            objSale.Id = intTempID;
            intTempID--;
        }
    }
}
```

Change the code to the code above.

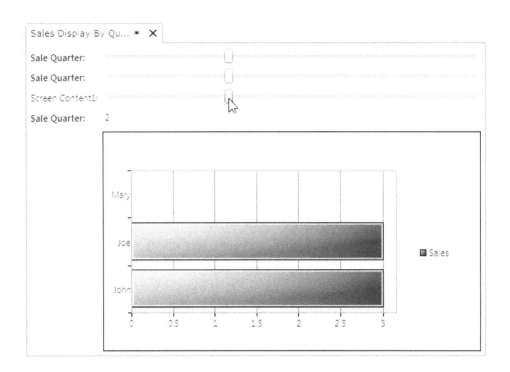

Now, when you run the application, Mary will show on the chart, even though she has no sales for the selected sale quarter.

Chapter 5: The Water Controller
"Calling Methods and Value Converters"

*Note: To complete the examples in this chapter, you will need **Microsoft Expression Blend 4** (or higher) see: http://www.microsoft.com/expression/products/blend_overview.aspx. If you do not have Expression Blend, you can download the completed code for this chapter from http://LightSwitchHelpWebsite.com.*

For the final project, we will create a LightSwitch application that will simulate a water management system. In real life, the water levels could be supplied by a WCF RIA Service; however, in this example we will just use random numbers.

The goal will be to not allow any tank to overflow past the level of 10.

- Pressing the **New Day** button will advance the system to a new "Day"
- The Main Tank will increase by a random amount each "Day"
- The City Tanks will decrease by a random amount each "Day"
- You can turn off flow to each City Tank from the Main Tank
- If the flow is turned on for both City Tanks, each City Tank will receive 50% of the flow from the Main Tank
- If only one City Tank is turned on, it will receive 100% of the flow from the Main Tank
- If both City Tanks are turned off, the flow for the day will remain in the Main Tank and be added to any existing flow in the Main Tank

This project will allow us to explore the use of Value Converters, and three methods of calling a method in LightSwitch from a Silverlight Custom Control.

Create The Water Controller Project

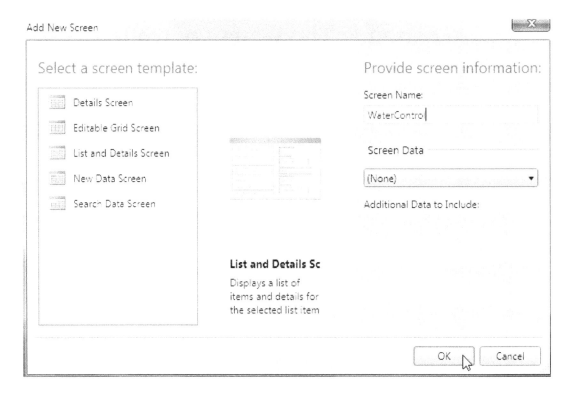

Create a new LightSwitch application called **WaterController**, and add a **List and Details Screen** (with no **Screen Data**) called **WaterControl**.

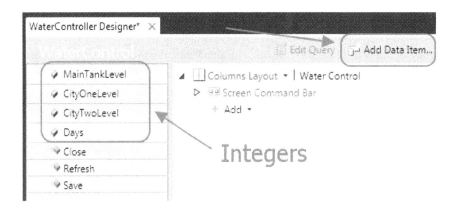

Use the **Add Data Item** button to add the properties above. Give them the type of **Integer**.

Use the **Add Data Item** button to add the properties above. Give them the type of **Boolean**

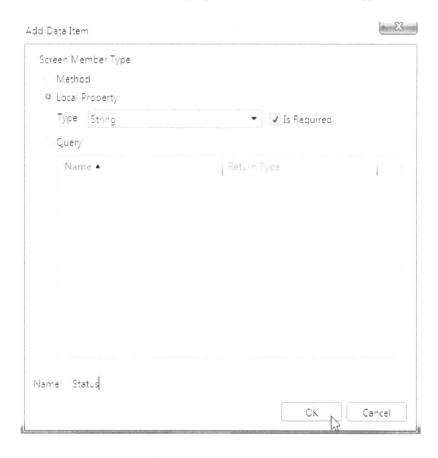

Use the **Add Data Item** button to add a **Status** property of type **String**.

In the Properties for the **Status** property, uncheck the **IS Required** box.

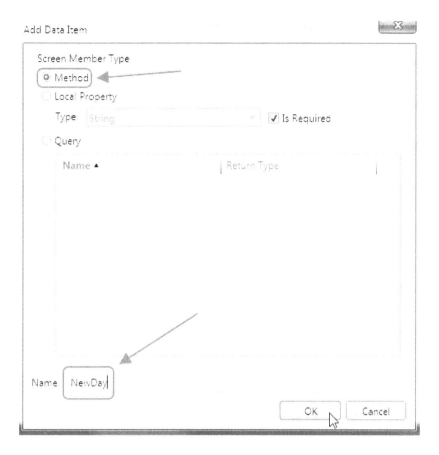

Create a **Method** called **NewDay**.

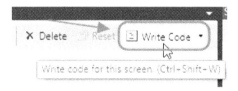

Click the **Write Code** button.

```
namespace LightSwitchApplication
{
    public partial class WaterControl
    {
        #region ResetGame
        private void ResetGame()
        {
            this.Status = "";
            this.Days = 0;

            this.MainTankLevel = 2;
            this.CityOneLevel = 0;
            this.CityTwoLevel = 0;

            this.CityOneFlowOn = true;
            this.CityTwoFlowOn = true;
        }
        #endregion

        #region RandomMainTankNumber
        private int RandomMainTankNumber()
        {
            Random random = new Random();
            return random.Next(2, 6);
        }
        #endregion

        #region RandomCityNumber
        private int RandomCityNumber()
        {
            Random random = new Random();
            return random.Next(1, 3);
        }
        #endregion
    }
}
```

Change the code to the code above.

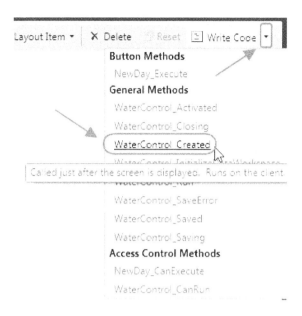

Switch back to the screen designer, and select **WaterControl_Created**.

```
partial void WaterControl_Created()
{
    ResetGame();
}
```

Use the code above.

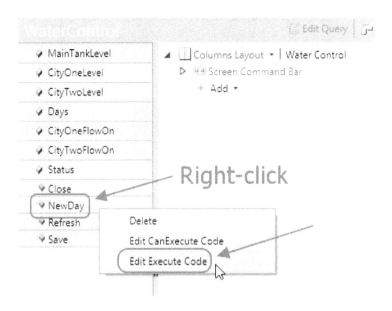

In the screen designer, on the *left-hand* side of the screen, *right-click* on the **NewDay** method, and select **Edit Execute Code**.

```
partial void NewDay_Execute()
{
    if (this.Status != "")
    {
        ResetGame();
    }

    this.Days++;

    // Increse Main Tank by a random number
    MainTankLevel = MainTankLevel + RandomMainTankNumber();

    // Decrease CityOneLevel by a random number
    CityOneLevel = CityOneLevel - RandomCityNumber();
    // Prevent CityOneLevel from being less than 0
    CityOneLevel = (CityOneLevel < 0) ? 0 : CityOneLevel;

    // Decrease CityTwoLevel by a random number
    CityTwoLevel = CityTwoLevel - RandomCityNumber();
    // Prevent CityTwoLevel from being less than 0
    CityTwoLevel = (CityTwoLevel < 0) ? 0 : CityTwoLevel;

}
```

Add the code above.

Add the following additional code to the **NewDay_Execute()** method:

```
// Add water to cities
if ((this.CityOneFlowOn) && (this.CityTwoFlowOn))
{
    CityOneLevel = CityOneLevel + (MainTankLevel / 2);
    MainTankLevel = MainTankLevel - (MainTankLevel / 2);
    CityTwoLevel = CityTwoLevel + MainTankLevel;
    MainTankLevel = 0;
}
else
{
    if (this.CityOneFlowOn)
    {
        CityOneLevel = CityOneLevel + MainTankLevel;
        MainTankLevel = 0;
    }

    if (this.CityTwoFlowOn)
    {
        CityTwoLevel = CityTwoLevel + MainTankLevel;
        MainTankLevel = 0;
    }
}

// Check for overflow

if (MainTankLevel > 10)
{
    this.Status =
        String.Format("Main Tank overflowed to {0}",
        MainTankLevel.ToString());
}

if (CityOneLevel > 10)
{
    this.Status =
        String.Format("City One Tank overflowed to {0}",
        CityOneLevel.ToString());
}

if (CityTwoLevel > 10)
{
    this.Status =
        String.Format("City Two Tank overflowed to {0}",
        CityTwoLevel.ToString());
}
```

Create The Silverlight Project

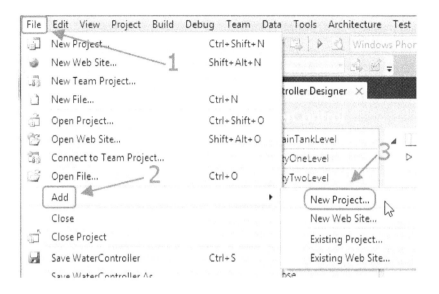

Add a **New Project**.

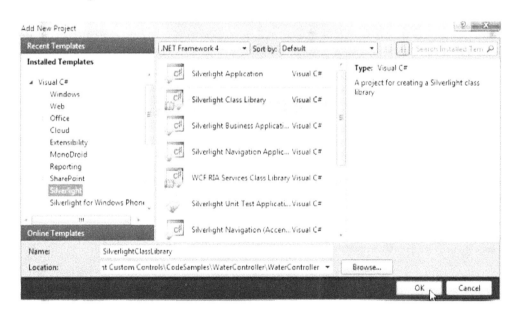

Make it a **Silverlight Class Library**. Name it **SilverlightClassLibrary**.

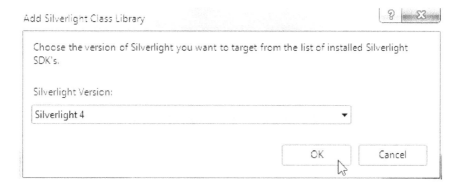

Make it a **Silverlight 4** project.

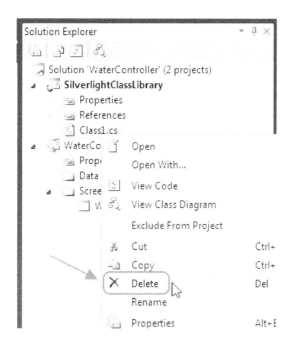

Delete the **Class1.cs** file that is created.

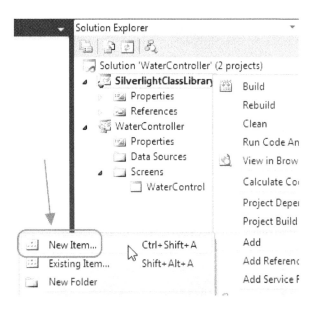

Add a **New Item**.

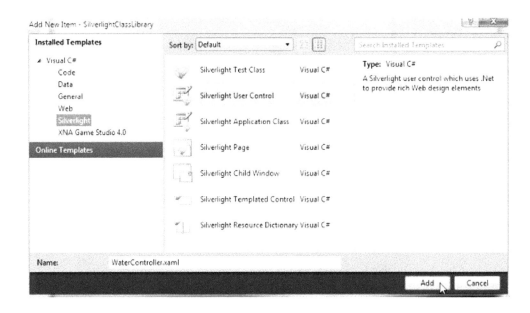

Add a new **Silverlight User Control** and name it **WaterController.xaml**.

```
<UserControl x:Class="SilverlightClassLibrary.WaterController"
    xmlns="http://schemas.microsoft.com/winfx/2006/xaml/presentation"
    xmlns:x="http://schemas.microsoft.com/winfx/2006/xaml"
    xmlns:d="http://schemas.microsoft.com/expression/blend/2008"
    xmlns:mc="http://schemas.openxmlformats.org/markup-compatibility/2006"
    mc:Ignorable="d" Height="392" Width="594">
    <Canvas x:Name="LayoutRoot" Background="White">
    </Canvas>
</UserControl>
```

Use the code for the control above.

```
<Rectangle Fill="#FFF4F4F5" Height="115" Canvas.Left="140"
           Stroke="Black" Canvas.Top="122" Width="98" RadiusX="39" RadiusY="3"/>

<Rectangle x:Name="Water" Fill="#FF10108D" Height="10" Canvas.Top="227" Canvas.Left="140"
           Stroke="Black" Width="98" RadiusX="39" StrokeThickness="0"/>
<TextBlock Height="17" Canvas.Left="260" TextWrapping="Wrap" Canvas.Top="85"
           Width="86" TextAlignment="Center" FontSize="10.667" FontWeight="Bold" Text="City One"/>
<TextBlock Height="17" Canvas.Left="370" TextWrapping="Wrap" Canvas.Top="85"
           Width="86" TextAlignment="Center" FontSize="10.667" FontWeight="Bold" Text="City Two"/>

<Rectangle Fill="#FFF4F4F5" Height="115" Canvas.Left="260" Stroke="Black" Canvas.Top="122"
           Width="86" RadiusX="39" RadiusY="3"/>
<Rectangle Fill="#FFF4F4F5" Height="115" Canvas.Left="370" Stroke="Black" Canvas.Top="122"
           Width="86" RadiusX="39" RadiusY="3"/>

<Rectangle x:Name="CityOneTank" Fill="#FF10108D" Height="10"    Canvas.Top="227" Canvas.Left="260"
           Stroke="Black" Width="86" RadiusX="39" StrokeThickness="0"/>
<Rectangle x:Name="CityTwoTank" Fill="#FF10108D" Height="10" Canvas.Top="227" Canvas.Left="370"
           Stroke="Black" Width="86" RadiusX="39" StrokeThickness="0"/>

<Rectangle Fill="#FF10108D" Height="19" Canvas.Left="177" Stroke="Black" Canvas.Top="237" Width="24"
           StrokeThickness="0"/>
<Rectangle Fill="#FF10108D" Height="9" Canvas.Left="201" RadiusX="39" Stroke="Black" Canvas.Top="247"
           Width="225" StrokeThickness="0"/>
<Rectangle Fill="#FF10108D" Height="19" Canvas.Left="293" RadiusX="39" Stroke="Black" Canvas.Top="237"
           Width="24" StrokeThickness="0"/>
<Rectangle Fill="#FF10108D" Height="19" Canvas.Left="402" RadiusX="39" Stroke="Black" Canvas.Top="237"
           Width="24" StrokeThickness="0"/>

<TextBlock Height="20" Canvas.Left="140" TextWrapping="Wrap" Canvas.Top="85" Width="98"
           TextAlignment="Center" FontSize="10.667" FontWeight="Bold" Text="Main Tank"/>

<TextBlock Height="17" Canvas.Left="370" TextWrapping="Wrap" Canvas.Top="102" Width="86"
           TextAlignment="Center" FontSize="10.667" FontWeight="Bold"
           Text="{Binding Screen.CityTwoLevel, FallbackValue=0}"/>
<TextBlock Height="17" Canvas.Left="260" TextWrapping="Wrap" Canvas.Top="101" Width="86"
           TextAlignment="Center" FontSize="10.667" FontWeight="Bold"
           Text="{Binding Screen.CityOneLevel, FallbackValue=0}"/>
<TextBlock Height="17" Canvas.Left="149" TextWrapping="Wrap" Canvas.Top="101" Width="86"
           TextAlignment="Center" FontSize="10.667" FontWeight="Bold"
           Text="{Binding Screen.MainTankLevel, FallbackValue=0}"/>

<TextBlock Height="17" Canvas.Left="140" TextWrapping="Wrap" Canvas.Top="53"
           Width="206" FontSize="10.667" FontWeight="Bold"
           Text="{Binding Screen.Status, FallbackValue='[status]'}" Foreground="Red"/>
<TextBlock Height="17" Canvas.Left="435" TextWrapping="Wrap" Canvas.Top="53"
           Width="21" FontSize="10.667" FontWeight="Bold"
           Text="{Binding Screen.Days, FallbackValue=0}" Foreground="Red"/>
<TextBlock Height="17" Canvas.Left="370" TextWrapping="Wrap" Canvas.Top="53"
           Width="56" TextAlignment="Right" FontSize="10.667" FontWeight="Bold"
           Text="Days: "/>
```

Enter the code above between the **Canvas** tags.

(Note: you can download the complete code from http://LightSwitchHelpWebsite.com)

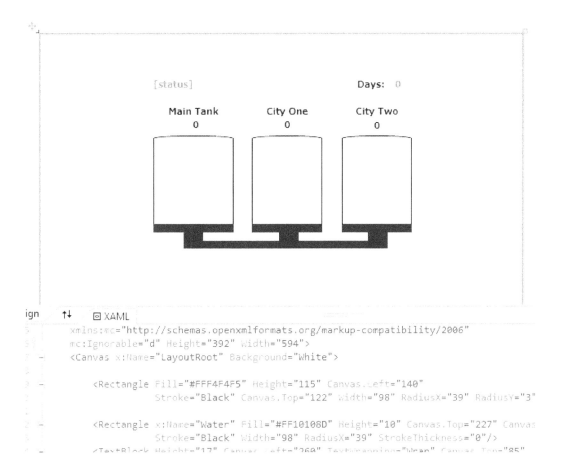

The screen will show up in the screen designer. At this point, it is a very simple screen with simple bindings.

Build the solution.

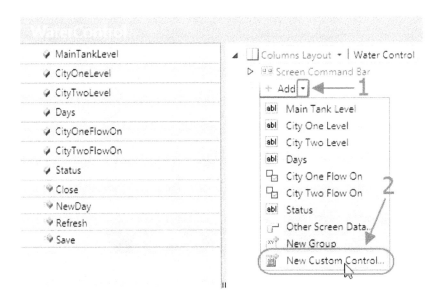

In the LightSwitch screen designer, select **New Custom Control**.

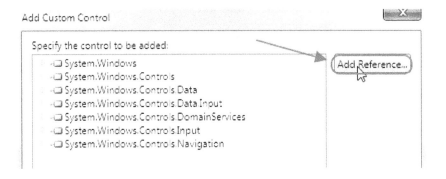

Add a **Reference**.

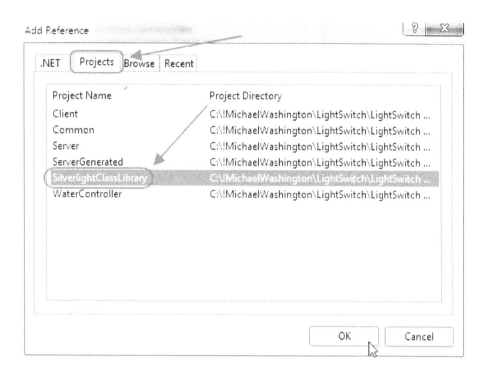

Select **Projects** then the **SilverlightClassLibrary** project.

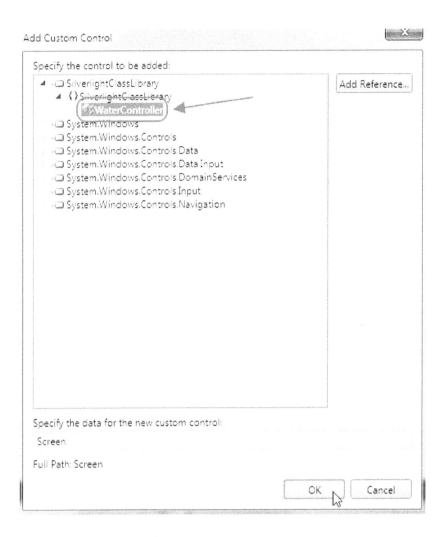

Select the **WaterController** control

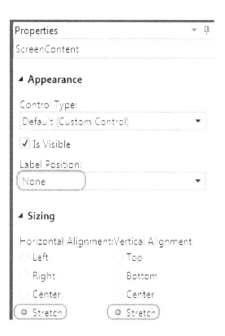

In the Properties for the control, set the **Label Position** to **None** and the **Alignment** to **Stretch**.

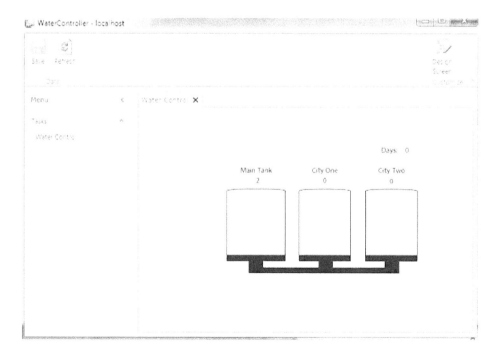

When you run the project, the control will show.

Calling Methods in LightSwitch From a Custom Control

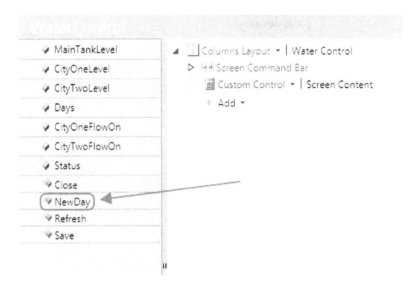

We now need a button to advance the "Day" in the program. We already have the method that will be called, **NewDay**.

We need to call that method from the Silverlight Custom Control.

We will explore two ways to call a method in LightSwitch from a Silverlight Custom Control.

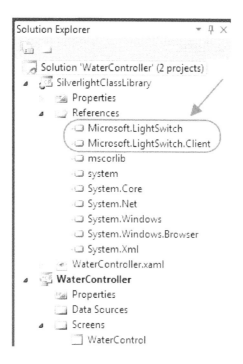

Both of the methods to call LightSwitch from a Silverlight Custom Control require references in the Silverlight project to:

- **Microsoft.LightSwitch** –
  ..\ClientGenerated\Bin\Debug\Microsoft.LightSwitch.dll
- **Microsoft.LightSwitch.Client** –
  ..\ClientGenerated\Bin\Debug\Microsoft.LightSwitch.Client.dll

We will add a button to the page, to allow us to call the **NewDay** method.

10 Cool Buttons for Download in Expression Blend & Silverlight

Licence
First Posted
Views
Downloads
Bookmarke

By Alan Beasley | 13 Jul 2010 | Unedited contribution

C# Windows WinMobile .NET Mobile XAML WPF Beginner Intermediate Silverlight

The WC Door button, covering all the missing skills needed to create the buttons shown in my 1st all 10 buttons for download!

Article Browse Code | Stats | Revisions (14) 4.95 (115 votes)

Introduction

Welcome to my fourth **Beginners** tutorial for **Expression Blend & Silverlight**.

And I ask for your vote, as I appear to be the only pure **Graphics**, or **Silverlight** styling person

So you decide if I should be here or not!!!!

All available for download & free use - Please vote!!!

We will use a button from the **Alan Beasley** project at:
http://www.codeproject.com/KB/expression/10FreeButtons.aspx.

(Note: you can also get free XAML controls from http://www.xamalot.com/)

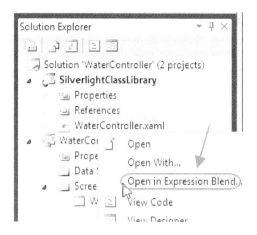

When working with graphics, it is recommended that you use **Microsoft Expression Blend 4** (or higher).

After you have installed **Expression Blend**, in the **Solution Explorer** in **Visual Studio**, *right-click* on the **WaterController.xaml** file, and select **Open in Expression Blend**.

You will see a message indicating that the LightSwitch project cannot be opened. This is not a problem because the Silverlight project will be opened.

Click the **Close** button.

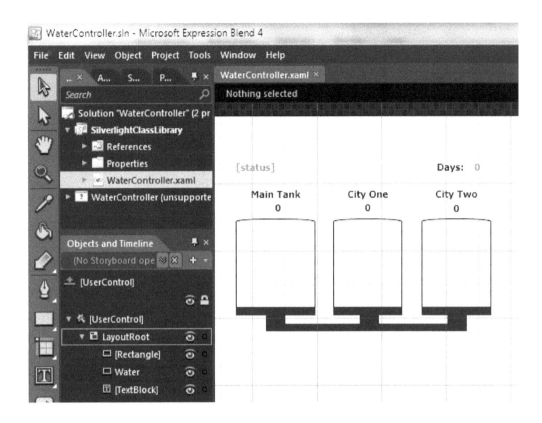

The Silverlight project will open in **Expression Blend**.

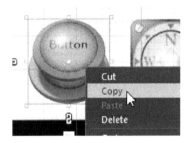

Open the **Alan Beasley Buttons10** project in a separate instance of **Expression Blend**, and copy the **PlungerButton**.

Paste it onto the **WaterController.xaml** page.

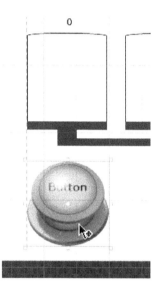

Drag the button to position it under the first tank.

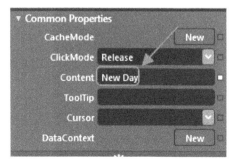

Click on the button, and in the Properties, change the **Content** to "**New Day**".

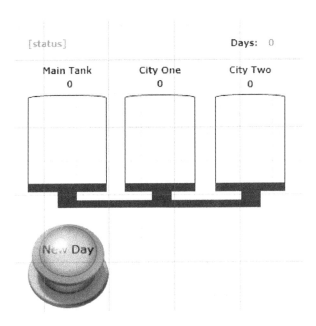

The button user interface is complete.

Method One: The Sheel Shah Method

The first method to raise a method in LightSwitch from a Silverlight Custom Control was presented by LightSwitch team member **Sheel Shah**.

In **Expression Blend**, save the project.

Open the **WaterController.xaml** page in **Visual Studio** (note that we are in **Visual Studio**, not in **Expression Blend**), and *double-click* on the button.

The code for the **WaterController.xaml.cs** file will open.

```csharp
using System.Windows;
using System.Windows.Controls;
using Microsoft.LightSwitch.Presentation;

namespace SilverlightClassLibrary
{
    public partial class WaterController : UserControl
    {
        public WaterController()
        {
            InitializeComponent();
        }

        private void PlungerButton_Click(object sender, RoutedEventArgs e)
        {
            // Get a reference to the LightSwitch DataContext
            var objDataContext = (IContentItem)this.DataContext;

            // Get a reference to the LightSwitch Screen
            var Screen =
                (Microsoft.LightSwitch.Client.IScreenObject)objDataContext.Screen;

            // Call the Method on the LightSwitch screen
            Screen.Details.Dispatcher.BeginInvoke(() =>
            {
                Screen.Details.Methods["NewDay"]
                    .CreateInvocation(null).Execute();
            });
        }
    }
}
```

Change the code to the code above.

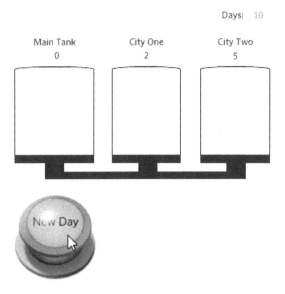

When you run the project, the **NewDay** method will be called when you click the button.

(Remember to switch back to a LightSwitch screen in the main LightSwitch project before trying to run the project. Otherwise you will get an error)

Method Two: The Karol Zadora-Przylecki Method

The second method to raise a method in LightSwitch from a Silverlight Custom Control was presented by LightSwitch team member **Karol Zadora-Przylecki**.

This method addresses a disadvantage of the first method, which is that the code can break (if the method signature changes), and it won't show up at compile-time.

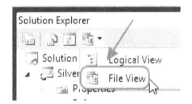

Click on the **WaterController** project in the **Solution Explorer**, and switch to **File View**.

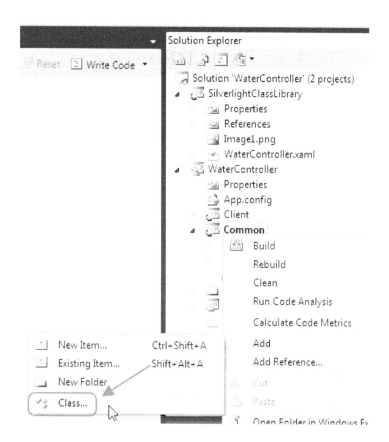

Add a new class to the **Common** project.

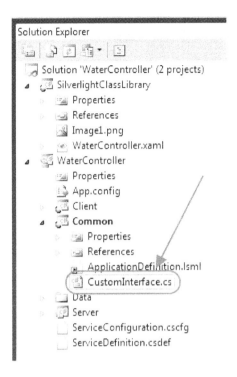

Call it **CustomInterface.cs**.

```
namespace LightSwitchApplication
{
    public interface IWaterController
    {
        void NewDay();
    }
}
```

Use the code above.

Build the solution.

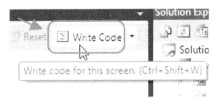

In the screen designer, select **Write Code**.

```
 6    using Microsoft.LightSwitch;
 7    using Microsoft.LightSwitch.Framework.Client;
 8    using Microsoft.LightSwitch.Presentation;
 9    using Microsoft.LightSwitch.Presentation.Extensions;
10  - namespace LightSwitchApplication
11    {
12        public partial class WaterControl : IWaterController
13        {
14            partial void WaterControl_Created()
15            {
16                ResetGame();
17            }
18
19  +         ResetGame
```

Add the Interface **IWaterController** to the class.

```
      using Microsoft.LightSwitch.Presentation.Extensions;
 2  - namespace LightSwitchApplication
 1    {
20        public partial class WaterControl : IWaterController                    1
      Implement Interface              ▸        Implement Interface Explicitly
      Refactor                         ▸      2
      Organize Usings                  ▸
```

Right-click on **IWaterController**, and implement the **Interface**.

```
                    void IWaterController.NewDay()
                    {
                        NewDay_Execute();
                    }
```

Use the code above.

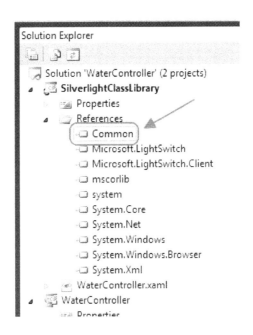

Add a **Reference** to the **Common** project in the **SilverlightClassLibrary** project.

```
private void PlungerButton_Click(object sender, RoutedEventArgs e)
{
    // Get a reference to the LightSwitch DataContext
    var objDataContext = (IContentItem)this.DataContext;

    // Get a reference to the LightSwitch Screen
    var Screen =
        (Microsoft.LightSwitch.Client.IScreenObject)objDataContext.Screen;

    // Cast the LightSwitch Screen to our custom Interface
    // (that we put in the "common" project)
    var IWaterController =
        (LightSwitchApplication.IWaterController)Screen;

    // Call the Method on the LightSwitch screen
    Screen.Details.Dispatcher.BeginInvoke(() =>
    {
        IWaterController.NewDay();
    });
}
```

Change the code in the **PlungerButton_Click** method, in the **WaterController.xaml.cs**, file to the code above.

When you run the project, the button will still work.

Method Three: The Joe Binder Method

The third method is called the Joe Binder method because he is the LightSwitch team member who insisted that there was no reason that this method should not work.

This method uses **Expression Blend Behaviors**, and is notable because it does not require any code behind in the Silverlight Custom Control.

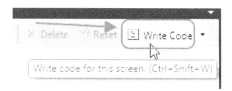

Open the **WaterControl** screen in the LightSwitch project and click the **Write Code** button.

```
public void proxyNewDay()
{
    this.Details.Dispatcher.BeginInvoke(() =>
    {
        NewDay_Execute();
    });
}
```

Enter the code above that provides a public method to call the **NewDay_Execute()** method, and wraps that call in **Dispatcher.BeginInvoke** so that the call is made on the proper thread.

Build the project.

First, we want to remove the code-behind code, and the click event, from the **New Day** button.

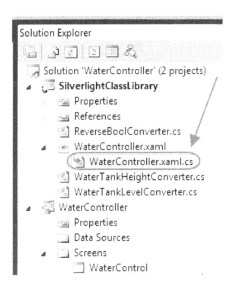

In the **Visual Studio Solution Explorer**, open the **WaterController.xaml.cs** file in the **SilverlightClassLibrary** project.

```
using Microsoft.LightSwitch.Presentation;

namespace SilverlightClassLibrary
{
    public partial class WaterController : UserControl
    {
        public WaterController()
        {
            InitializeComponent();
        }

        private void PlungerButton_Click(object sender, RoutedEventArgs e)
        {
            // Get a reference to the LightSwitch DataContext
            var objDataContext = (IContentItem)this.DataContext;

            // Get a reference to the LightSwitch Screen
            var Screen =
                (Microsoft.LightSwitch.Client.IScreenObject)objDataContext.Screen;

            // Cast the LightSwitch Screen to our custom Interface
            // (that we put in the "common" project)
            var IWaterController =
                (LightSwitchApplication.IWaterController)Screen;

            // Call the Method on the LightSwitch screen
            Screen.Details.Dispatcher.BeginInvoke(() =>
            {
                IWaterController.NewDay();
            });
        }
    }
}
```

Delete

Delete the **PlungerButton_Click** method and save the page.

Open the **WaterController.xaml** page in the **Expression Blend** designer.

Click on the **New Day** button. In the Properties for the button, click on the **Events** button, and highlight and *delete* the **Click** method (we already deleted the code-behind that this would have called).

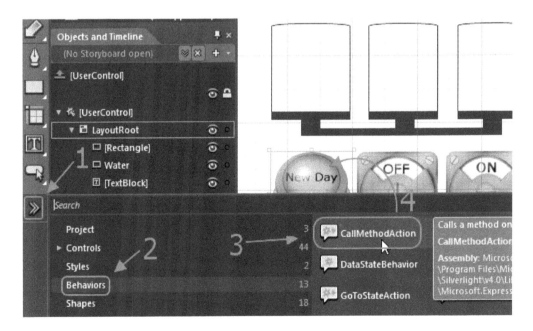

Grab a **CallMethodAction** Behavior and drag it and drop it on the **New Day** button.

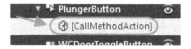

The Behavior will appear below the button in the **Objects and Timeline** window.

In the Properties for the Behavior, select **Advanced options** for **Target Object**.

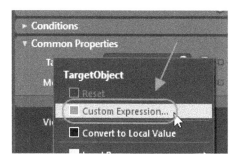

Select **Custom Expression**.

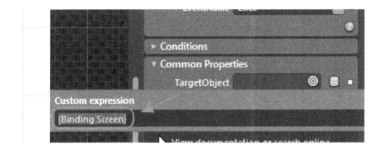

Enter {**Binding Screen**}.

This sets the LightSwitch screen as the target.

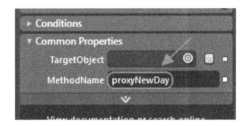

Enter **proxyNewDay** for **MethodName**.

This will call the method that we created. Save the page.

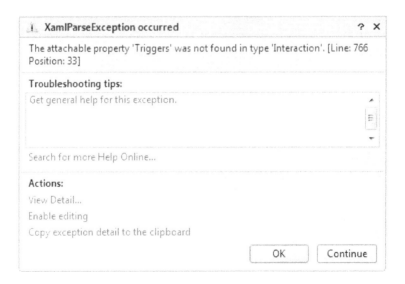

If we try to run the project at this point we would get an error.

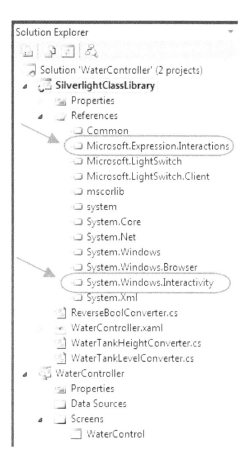

The reason the project won't run at this point, is that our recent actions automatically added the following references to the Silverlight project:

- Microsoft.Expression.Interactions
- System.Windows.Interactivity

These need to be added to the LightSwitch project.

We will not add them as we would a normal **Visual Studio** project; we will add them in the LightSwitch UI, because that will add them to the important LightSwitch manifest files.

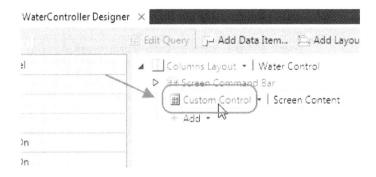

Open the **WaterController** screen in **Visual Studio**, click on the **Custom Control**.

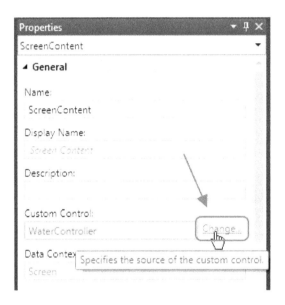

In the Properties for the **Custom Control**, click the **Change** button.

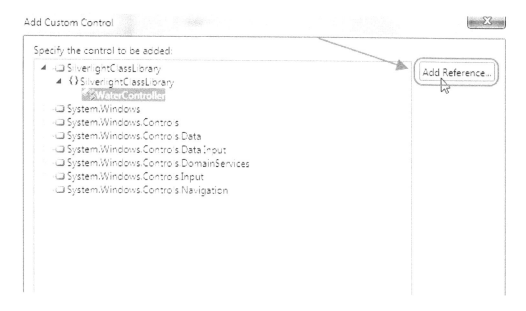

We only did that to get to the **Add Reference** button. Click it.

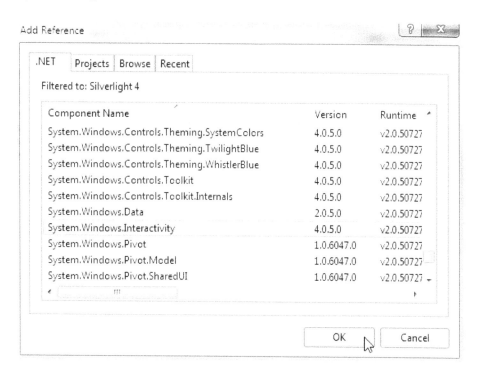

Add references to

- Microsoft.Expression.Interactions
- System.Windows.Interactivity

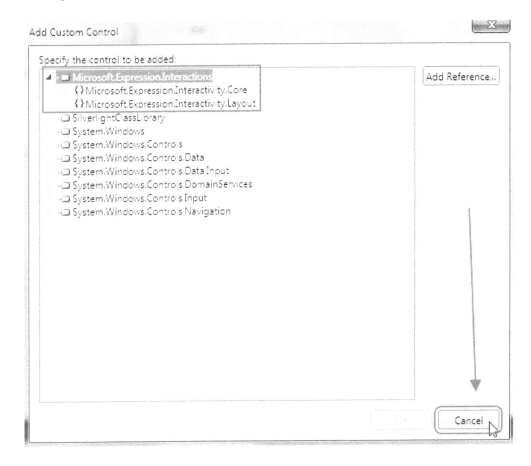

Click the **Cancel** button (because we only wanted to add the references not actually change the **Silverlight Custom Control**).

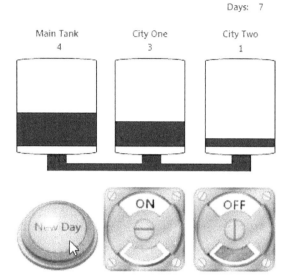

Now when we run the application it works.

Value Converters

The first question you may have is, why do you need value converters? Value converters are classes that you create, that implement the **IValueConverter** Interface.

According to http://MSDN.Microsoft.com, the IValueConverter Interface "Exposes methods that allow modifying the data as it passes through the binding engine".

What this means, is that a value converter allows you to convert a value, into a different value that can be consumed for a particular situation.

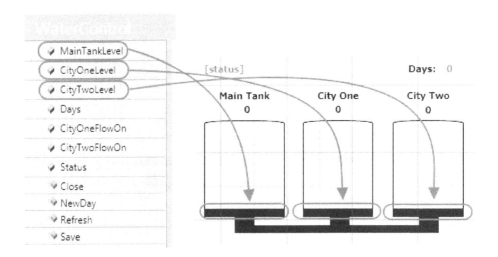

For example, we need to show the level in each of the tanks. The value we have is an integer (**MainTankLevel**, **CityOneLevel**, and **CityTwoLevel**).

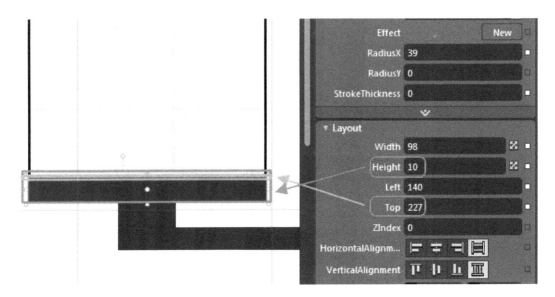

We need this converted to two different values. One for the location of the top of the graphic, that represents the water level (in relationship to the Canvas that it is on), and one for the height of the graphic (for this, the visual height of the water level object increases, as the Canvas.Top value of the water level object decreases).

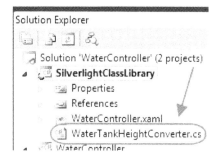

In the **SilverlightClassLibrary** project, add a class called **WaterTankHeightConverter.cs**.

```csharp
using System;
using System.Windows.Data;

namespace SilverlightClassLibrary
{
    public class WaterTankHeightConverter : IValueConverter
    {
        #region IValueConverter Members

        public object Convert(object value, Type targetType,
            object parameter, System.Globalization.CultureInfo culture)
        {
            int intLevel = (int)value;
            if (intLevel > 0)
            {
                return (227 + ((intLevel * 10) * -1));
            }
            else
            {
                return 0;
            }
        }

        public object ConvertBack(object value, Type targetType,
            object parameter, System.Globalization.CultureInfo culture)
        {
            throw new NotImplementedException(
                GetType().Name + "ConvertBack not implemented");
        }

        #endregion
    }
}
```

Use the code above.

Only the **Convert** method of the **IValueConverter** interface is fully implemented, the **ConvertBack** method is not.

The **Convert** method takes the value passed to it and multiplies it by 10 and adds 227 to the value (you will note in the earlier graphic that 227 is the top of the water object when the water level is at 1). The final value is multiplied by -1 to produce a negative number (Canvas.Top needs to decrease for the height of the water to grow).

In the **SilverlightClassLibrary** project, add a class called **WaterTankHeightConverter.cs**.

```csharp
using System;
using System.Windows.Data;

namespace SilverlightClassLibrary
{
    public class WaterTankLevelConverter : IValueConverter
    {
        #region IValueConverter Members

        public object Convert(object value, Type targetType,
            object parameter, System.Globalization.CultureInfo culture)
        {
            int intLevel = (int)value;
            if (intLevel > 0)
            {
                return (intLevel * 10);
            }
            else
            {
                return 0;
            }
        }

        public object ConvertBack(object value, Type targetType,
            object parameter, System.Globalization.CultureInfo culture)
        {
            throw new NotImplementedException(
                GetType().Name + "ConvertBack not implemented");
        }

        #endregion
    }
}
```

Use the code above.

```xaml
1  - <UserControl x:Class="SilverlightClassLibrary.WaterController"
2        xmlns="http://schemas.microsoft.com/winfx/2006/xaml/presentation"
3        xmlns:x="http://schemas.microsoft.com/winfx/2006/xaml"
4        xmlns:d="http://schemas.microsoft.com/expression/blend/2008"
5        xmlns:mc="http://schemas.openxmlformats.org/markup-compatibility/2006"
6        xmlns:local="clr-namespace:SilverlightClassLibrary"
7        mc:Ignorable="d" Height="392" Width="594">
8  -     <UserControl.Resources>
9            <local:WaterTankLevelConverter x:Key="WaterTankLevelConverter"/>
10           <local:WaterTankHeightConverter x:Key="WaterTankHeightConverter"/>
11 -         <Style TargetType="Button" x:Key="PlungerButton">
12               <Setter Property="Background" Value="#FF587A58"/>
13               <Setter Property="Foreground" Value="Black"/>
14               <Setter Property="Padding" Value="0"/>
15               <Setter Property="BorderThickness" Value="1"/>
16               <Setter Property="BorderBrush" Value="Lime"/>
17 -             <Setter Property="Template">
18 -                 <Setter.Value>
19 -                     <ControlTemplate TargetType="Button">
```

100 % ▾

☑ XAML   ↑↓   ⬜ Design

[status]   Da

Main Tank   City One   Cit

First, we need to add a reference to the value converters in the XAML file. Add the highlighted code to the **WaterController.xaml** file.

```xaml
<Rectangle Fill="#FFF4F4F5" Height="115" Canvas.Left="140" Stroke="Black" Canvas.Top

<Rectangle x:Name="Water" Fill="#FF10108D"
Height="{Binding Screen.MainTankLevel,
    Converter={StaticResource WaterTankLevelConverter}, FallbackValue=10}"
Canvas.Top="{Binding Screen.MainTankLevel,
    ConverterParameter=227,
    Converter={StaticResource WaterTankHeightConverter}, FallbackValue=227}"
Canvas.Left="140" Stroke="Black" Width="98" RadiusX="39" StrokeThickness="0"/>

<ToggleButton x:Name="CityOneSwitch" Content="Button" Height="87" Canvas.Left="260"
```

Change the code for the "**Water**" Rectangle to the code above.

```
<Rectangle Fill="#FFF4F4F5" Height="113" Canvas.Left="370" Stroke="Black" Canvas.Top=
         Width="86" RadiusX="39" RadiusY="3"/>
```

```
<Rectangle x:Name="CityOneTank" Fill="#FF10108D"
    Height="{Binding Screen.CityOneLevel,
    Converter={StaticResource WaterTankLevelConverter}, FallbackValue=10}"
    Canvas.Top="{Binding Screen.CityOneLevel,
    ConverterParameter=227,
    Converter={StaticResource WaterTankHeightConverter}, FallbackValue=227}"
    Canvas.Left="260" Stroke="Black" Width="86" RadiusX="39" StrokeThickness="0"/>
```

```
<Rectangle x:Name="CityTwoTank" Fill="#FF10108D"
    Height="{Binding Screen.CityTwoLevel,
    Converter={StaticResource WaterTankLevelConverter}, FallbackValue=10}"
    Canvas.Top="{Binding Screen.CityTwoLevel,
    ConverterParameter=227,
    Converter={StaticResource WaterTankHeightConverter}, FallbackValue=227}"
    Canvas.Left="370" Stroke="Black" Width="86" RadiusX="39" StrokeThickness="0"/>
```

```
<Rectangle Fill="#FF10108D" Height="19" Canvas.Left="177" Stroke="Black" Canvas.Top=
```

Change the code for the "**CityOneTank**" and the "**CityTwoTank**" Rectangles to the code above.

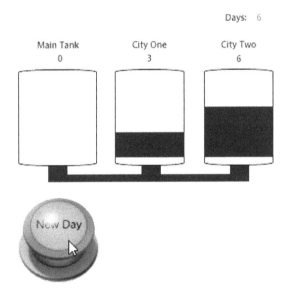

When you run the application, the water levels will change in the tanks.

Finishing Touches

To complete the project, we will add **Toggle** controls to turn off the water flow to the City Tanks.

First, we need to add a **ReverseBoolConverter.cs** file to the **SilverlightClassLibrary** project.

```
using System;
using System.Windows;
using System.Windows.Data;

namespace SilverlightClassLibrary
{
    public class ReverseBoolConverter : IValueConverter
    {
        #region IValueConverter Members

        public object Convert(object value, Type targetType,
            object parameter, System.Globalization.CultureInfo culture)
        {
            return (!(bool)value);
        }

        public object ConvertBack(object value, Type targetType,
            object parameter, System.Globalization.CultureInfo culture)
        {
            return (!(bool)value);
        }

        #endregion
    }
}
```

Use the code above.

The control that we will use is a Toggle control, but its toggle states are the reverse from what we ultimately want. This value converter fixes that. You will run into problems like this with other controls, and a value converter is always your answer.

Also note that this value converter does implement both the **Convert** and **ConvertBack** methods (because the value can be changed both by the Toggle control and by LightSwitch programmatically).

```
xmlns:local="clr-namespace:SilverlightClassLibrary"
mc:Ignorable="d" Height="392" Width="594">
<UserControl.Resources>
    <local:WaterTankLevelConverter x:Key="WaterTankLevelConverter"/>
    <local:WaterTankHeightConverter x:Key="WaterTankHeightConverter"/>
    <local:ReverseBoolConverter x:Key="ReverseBoolConverter"/>
    <Style TargetType="Button" x:Key="PlungerButton">
        <Setter Property="Background" Value="#FF587A58"/>
```

We also need to add a reference to the value converter in the .xaml file. To do this, add the highlighted code above, to the **WaterController.xaml** file.

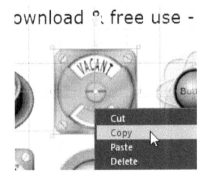

From the **Alan Beasley** project, copy the **WCDoorToggleButton**.

Paste it into the **SilverlightClassLibrary** project (in **Expression Blend**) twice.

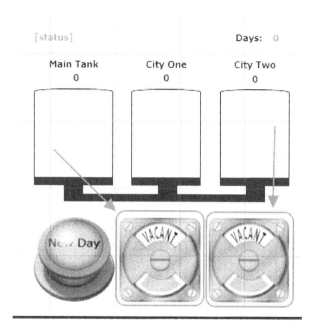

Drag each control, and position each according to the image above.

```
...LayoutOverrides="horizontalAlignment" Click="PlungerButton_Click" />

<ToggleButton x:Name="WCDoorToggleButton" Style="{StaticResource WCDoorToggleButton}"
  IsChecked="{Binding Screen.CityOneIsOn,
  Converter={StaticResource ReverseBoolConverter}, FallbackValue=false, Mode=TwoWay}"
  Height="100" Canvas.Left="246" Canvas.Top="275" Width="100"/>

<ToggleButton x:Name="WCDoorToggleButton_Copy" Style="{StaticResource WCDoorToggleButton}"
  IsChecked="{Binding Screen.CityTwoIsOn,
  Converter={StaticResource ReverseBoolConverter}, FallbackValue=false, Mode=TwoWay}"
  Height="100" Canvas.Left="356" Canvas.Top="275" Width="100"/>
</Canvas>
```

Add the binding code for the **IsChecked** property for each control, according to the code above.

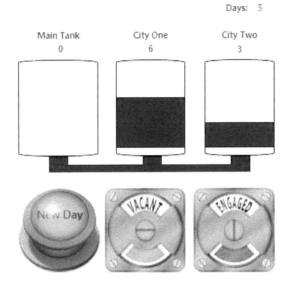

When we run the project, it now works.

However, the **Toggle** controls are labeled **Vacant** and **Engaged** and that is not appropriate for this situation.

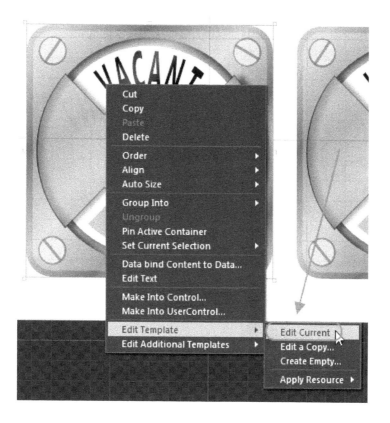

Return to **Expression Blend**, *right-click* on one of the Toggle controls, and select **Edit Current**.

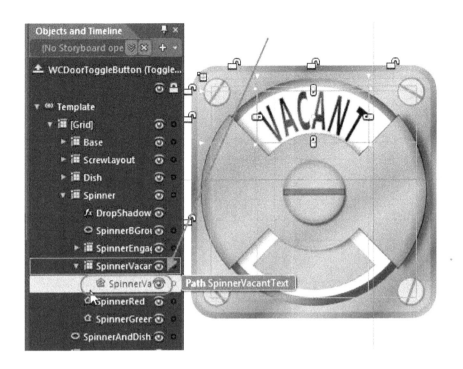

In the **Objects and Timeline** window, select the **SpinnerVacantText**.

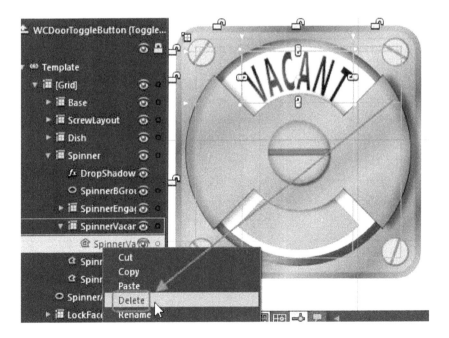

Right-click on it to **Delete** it.

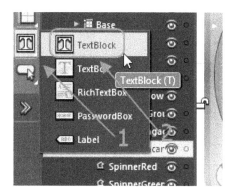

On the Toolbar, select the **TextBlock** tool.

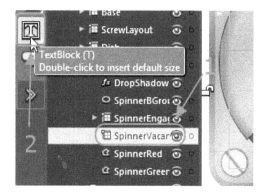

Click on the **SpinnerVacant** Grid and *double-click* on **TextBlock** in the Toolbar, to place a **TextBlock** inside the **SpinnerVacant** Grid.

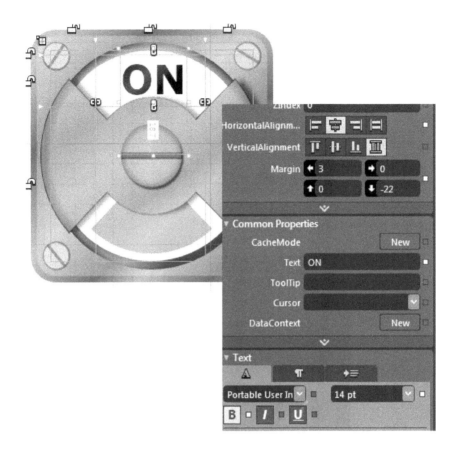

Use the Selection tool to reposition the **TextBlock**, and set the Properties according to the image above.

All changes will automatically be reflected in both instances of the Toggle control, because they share the same *style template* (see: http://msdn.microsoft.com/en-us/library/cc296245(v=vs.95).aspx for more information on Style Templates).

Click **Eye** symbol next to **LockFace** in the **Objects and Timeline** window, to allow visual access to the **Engaged** text.

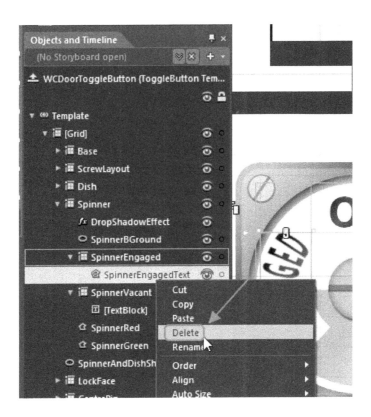

Delete **SpinnerEngagedText**.

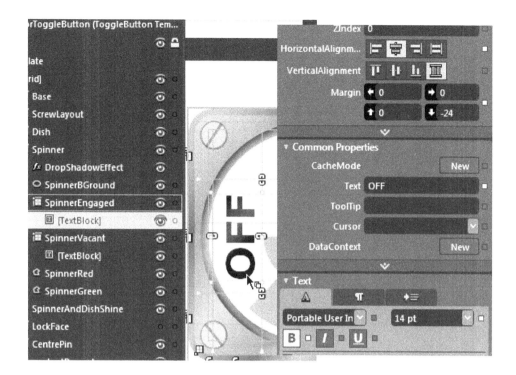

Click on the **SpinnerEngaged** Grid and *double-click* on **TextBlock** in the Toolbar, to place a **TextBlock** inside the **SpinnerEngaged** Grid.

Use the Selection tool to reposition the **TextBlock**, and set the properties according to the image above.

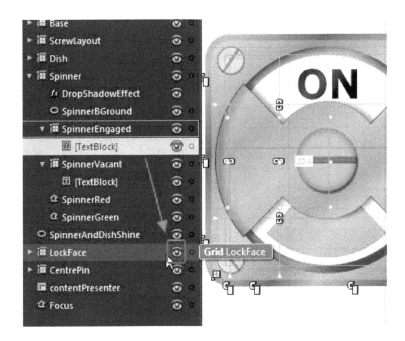

Click **Eye** symbol next to **LockFace** in the **Objects and Timeline** window, to redisplay the element.

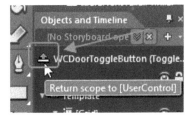

Select the **Return Scope** button.

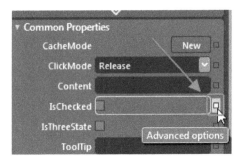

Select the Toggle control, and in the Properties, select the **Advanced options** next to **IsChecked**.

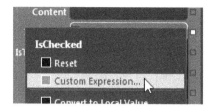

Select **Custom Expression**.

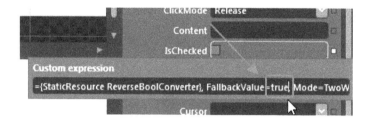

Change the **FallbackValue** to **true**.

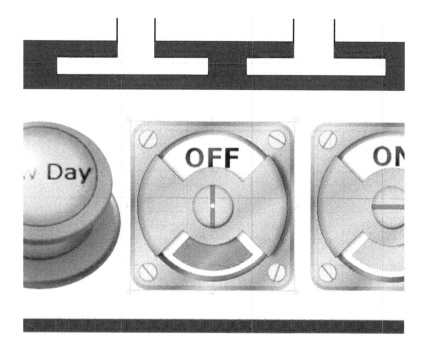

This will cause the **Toggle** control to switch to its other state so you can check the result.

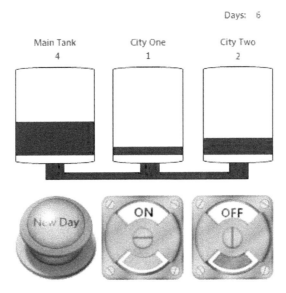

When you run the program, you will see that the application is complete.

Chapter 6
"Onward"

There is still a lot more to creating Custom Controls for LightSwitch.

```
private void PlungerButton_Click(object sender, RoutedEventArgs e)
{
    // Get a reference to the LightSwitch DataContext
    var objDataContext = (IContentItem)this.DataContext;

    objDataContext.|
                        ⚙ CommandItems
    // Get a refere    ⚙ ContainerState
    var Screen =        ⚙ ContentItemDefinition         objDataContext.Screen;
        (Microsoft.     ⚙ ContentItemKind
                        ⚙ CreateTemplatedTreeCopy       erface
    // Cast the Lig
    // (that we put     ⚙ DataError
    var IWaterContr     ⚙ DataSourceRoot                System.Exception IContentItem.DataError
        (LightSwitc     ⚙ DataSourceRootDefinition      een;
                        ⚙ Description
    // Call the Met
    Screen.Details.Dispatcher.BeginInvoke(() =>
```

For example, there are a number of properties and methods on the **DataContext** that we could consume for added functionality, such as tooltips and error displays within our custom controls.

```
    // Get a reference to the LightSwitch Screen
    var Screen =
        (Microsoft.LightSwitch.Client.IScreenObject)objDataContext.Screen;

    Screen.Details.
                        ⚙ Methods
    // Cast the Lig     ⚙ Name                          Interface
    // (that we put     ⚙ Owner
    var IWaterContr     ⚙ Properties                    )Screen;
        (LightSwitc     ⚙ SaveChangesTo
                        ⚙ Screen
    rverValidationResults  ⚙ ServerValidationResults
                        ⚙ ToString
```

The ability to reference the **Screen** and its various properties and methods, opens a world of possibilities. However, LightSwitch employs an underlying mechanism called "dual threading" that may require careful choices when implementing more complex controls.

For more information, see: **Using Custom Controls to Enhance LightSwitch Application UI** by **Karol Zadora-Przylecki** in **Code Magazine** (2011 Jul/Aug) http://www.code-magazine.com/article.aspx?quickid=1108091.

For an example of using custom controls with paging see: **Display a chart built on aggregated data** by **Eric Erhardt**)http://blogs.msdn.com/b/lightswitch/archive/2011/04/08/how-do-i-display-a-chart-built-on-aggregated-data-eric-erhardt.aspx).

About The Author

Michael Washington is an ASP.NET, C#, and Visual Basic programmer. He has extensive knowledge in process improvement, billing systems, and student information systems. He is a Microsoft Silverlight MVP. He has a son, Zachary and resides in Los Angeles with his wife Valerie.

www.ingramcontent.com/pod-product-compliance
Lightning Source LLC
Chambersburg PA
CBHW080426060326
40689CB00019B/4392